game-generating-games

By the same authors:

Gaming-Simulation: *Rationale, Design, and Applications*
Edited by Cathy S. Greenblat and Richard D. Duke

Gaming: *The Future's Language*
by Richard D. Duke

Published by Sage Publications and distributed by Halsted Press

game-generating-games

games

a trilogy of games for community and classroom

Richard D. Duke
and
Cathy S. Greenblat

SAGE PUBLICATIONS   Beverly Hills   London

For information address:

SAGE PUBLICATIONS, INC.
275 South Beverly Drive
Beverly Hills, California 90212

SAGE PUBLICATIONS LTD
28 Banner Street
London EC1Y 8QE, England

Printed in the United States of America

Library of Congress Cataloging in Publication Data

Duke, Richard D
  Game-generating-games.

  1. Game theory. 2. Social sciences—Simulation methods. 3. Simulation games in education.
I. Greenblat, Cathy S., 1940-   joint author.
II. Title.
H61.D84   300'.1'8   79-15721
ISBN 0-8039-1282-X

FIRST PRINTING

TABLE OF CONTENTS

LIST OF FIGURES

ACKNOWLEDGEMENTS

The three games presented here are "kissing cousins," at least in concept. They were initially developed by the authors for different but related purposes.

IMPASSE? was first developed by Duke and Greenblat for Radius International; the Rapid Transit IMPASSE? version was created for the National Museum of Design, Smithsonian Institute, as a citizen-participation device. Other versions have subsequently been developed and used in Hawaii, California, New York, Canada, South American and Europe by a cariety of groups.

AT-ISSUE! was developed by the authors for the Environmental Simulation Laboratory, The University of Michigan. Its first application was for the Council of Monterey Bay, under funding from the National Science Foundation. (The example presented here is adapted from one which was developed for citizen use in Monterey Bay by Richard D. Duke).

THE CONCEPTUAL MAPPING GAME...emerged from a logic developed in GAMING: THE FUTURE'S LANGUAGE, Richard D. Duke, Halsted Press, 1974. The example illustrating REGIONAL PLANNING, included here, was developed by Duke et al. for use in the Monterey Bay Project. Procedures for use of the game were more fully developed at the time.

Work by Richard D. Duke on the manuscript during the period January-July 1974 was supported by the Netherlands Institute for Advanced Study at which he was a fellow.

Richard D. Duke
University of Michigan
Ann Arbor, Michigan

Cathy S. Greenblat
Douglass College, Rutgers University
New Brunswick, New Jersey

November 1978

I. INTRODUCTION

Gaming-simulation is a relatively recent phenomenon, appearing in the social sciences only within the past decade. It has, however, gained rapid acceptance and its various forms can now be found in widespread use. There have been three basic uses of gaming-simulation: research, education, and public policy. Gaming-simulation has been employed for research and for many educational purposes since before World War II. The technique has been widely employed for educational purposes over the past decade, and we are entering a period in which we can expect to see wide dissemination and effective use of gaming-simulation in applied public policy contexts for citizen participation.

In both classroom and community contexts, games are a viable alternative to the audience-lecturer format for discussing problems. To be sure, they are a supplement and not a replacement, but their use permits interactive participation in an organized discussion of complex problems and issues. Contrast this with the formal lecturer-audience pattern where most of the participants are forced to become inactive "sponges" or, alternatively, are permitted to speak only in turn, as time permits. The game format is more spontaneous and creates a better ambience for dialogue.

One reason for this is that games are designed to get *you* involved, in their play as well as in their design. There are several reasons for this, but three are central:

> 1. You are required to take a role and argue the problem from that posture. If the roles are carefully selected, a balanced and spirited discussion ensues. Even though you may be playing

"devil's advocate" in your role, your understanding of the problem will be heightened.

2. Games organize complex details into an overview model. This allows the player to grasp details that might otherwise be lost. Discussion within this framework allows players to retain the major elements of the model for future reference.

3. Games require trial decisions, and this commitment sharpens the thought processes of the participants who are required to act. In the subsequent defense of those decisions, the players benefit from a more focused discussion.

You get deeply involved in building a game, too, but for different reasons. When you put a game together - for example, you put your problem into the IMPASSE? wheel - you have to organize your thoughts, with the knowledge that you'll have to defend these during the play of the game. If several people work together in game design each is forced to learn more about how the others perceive the problem.

The next section presents three basic frame games for citizen participation or student participation in organized discussions. They are called frame games because they are basic mechanisms or frameworks which can be loaded with appropriate subject matter for any occasion. The basic rules, once learned, persist for use after use, even though the subject matter changes. For example, a very simple frame game known to most of you is the crossword puzzle. The format is the same in every day's newspaper, but the content changes from day to day. In the case of the games presented here, the format is more sophisticated and more useful for classroom and community use, but the style is comparable.

The series of games presented here are currently in use in a wide variety of places. A quick glimpse at some of these might be helpful in giving you a feel for their possible use:

On the island of Oahu, Hawaii, a group of planners were working with other scientists and various citizen groups attempting to develop plans to cope with the rapid urbanization of this tiny dot in the Pacific. To improve communication (in both directions) between the scientist and the layman, as well as to elicit the support of community leaders, several versions of IMPASSE? were developed and used. They became tools for passing information along to lay groups, but more importantly, they were used as "questionaires" to find out how the citizens felt about proposals.

In California, a League of Women Voters group met to consider a new development being proposed in their town. Arriving with maps and reports and supported by several local "experts" they played AT-ISSUE! as a way of organizing their half-day meeting session.

Some of the county commisioners in Monterey Bay met to vote on a highway proposed to enter their region. A small group of them had studied the proposal in advance of the meeting, using the CONCEPTUAL MAPPING GAME...: REGIONAL PLANNING. Contrary to expectations, the commissioners voted against the proposed road. In a subsequent conversation one is quoted as saying "the deeper we got into that game, the more troubled I became. It became increasingly clear that this new road, if developed, would generate a whole array of new problems that we are not prepared to deal with at present."

In a freshman "survey" course in urban studies, a university professor required students to prepare trial versions of IMPASSE? to help them organize their thoughts and as a prod to encourage them to tackle a long reading list. As a result, class participation was spirited and the students had a permanent record of the discussion in the form of a set of simple games.

A high school teacher in the midwest, teaching a class on communications, had students load IMPASSE? with varying topics of interest. The interactive mode of communication caught on and a series of other IMPASSE? games designed by the students were published in the school newspaper.

The Philadelphia branch of the World Affairs Council sent an announcement of a meeting at which the issue of possible impeachment of President Nixon was to be discussed to some 2000 people. The announcement included a copy of the large wheel for IMPEACHMENT IMPASSE?, a version designed by David Rosen and the two authors of the original game. Recipients were encouraged to play the game at home and to come to the meeting to hear experts debate the answers that should be in the small wheel.

These are just a few examples to illustrate the range of potential use. The games are used in various combinations that require from an hour to a day. In some cases they are loaded with content in advance; in other instances, the participants are required to provide the content. By selecting the content with care, audiences ranging in sophistication from high school students to community leaders are accomodated.

The examples offered here are simply to illustrate how others have used the games, and to get you started on your own problem. We urge a simple procedure when you begin:

1. Learn how to play one of the games (section II).

2. Play it with a small group who are interested in the technique.

3. Learn how to build your own game (section III).

4. Make your own game.

5. Test and modify it.

6. Put it into use.

7. Repeat steps 1-6 with another of the games.

We encourage you to start with IMPASSE? and then try AT-ISSUE! before getting into the CONCEPTUAL MAPPING GAME...

This book is designed *to be used*, not read in the traditional sense. This short introduction is followed by an explanation of the three games in Section II. You are encouraged to play them, with as much gusto as possible, as soon as possible. The introductions are deliberately brief and nothing is required to play except the materials in the manual and pencils or pens, scissors and tape.

While several examples of loaded games are included, the intention of the manual is to encourage the development of new versions of the games to meet specific problems that you may have. Blank forms are provided for that purpose in the final section. In viewing the games included as examples, remember that they are only here as illustrations, or as a "starter set" to permit ready access to the technique.

In section III, the emphasis is on your designing your own version of the games, rather than reading about or playing the games. Section IV offers suggestions concerning the dissemination of your versions.

In section V you will find a copy of each of the examples offered here. Play with a large group will require that you reproduce more forms.

Finally, in section VI, blanks are provided for you to use in making your own games.

II. PLAYING THE GAMES

OVERVIEW OF THE THREE GAMES

The three games that follow are, in a sense, three versions of the same game, each successively more complicated. These initial examples each address some particular topic or problem. While playing them, remember that you can replace the content with any other topic or problem of interest to you.

The style in all three games is to present a problem (or issue, or alternative) and to have you consider the implications for a set of related factors (e.g. If you do this, what does it mean in terms of A, what does it mean in terms of B, and so on). The technique varies from game to game because the degree of complexity varies. IMPASSE? uses 30 variables; AT-ISSUE! uses 60; and CONCEPTUAL MAPPING GAME... uses several hundred.

In all cases the steps of play are simple, and no fancy equipment is required. You will need scissors and pencils for IMPASSE?; pencils for AT-ISSUE! colored flow pens and scissors for the CONCEPTUAL MAPPING GAME...

But first and foremost, *play the games!* The instructions always make them sound more difficult and involved than they really are. For example, do you remember MONOPOLY? Most of us learned to enjoy it by just sitting down and getting started. Only after we were "into" it and ran into trouble did we try to find our way through the long list of rules.

Remember, all three of these games are designed to improve the quality of group discussions about serious and complicated problems. *Therefore, there are no hard and fast rules of play!* Rather, you as a user should consider the instructions as suggested procedures which are known to be workable. You should change these procedures whenever some other device seems more workable for your purpose.

The next page lists the basic characteristics of the trilogy of games. Each was developed with a different problem situation in mind. Thus, you should review the characteristics as presented in the chart to determine which might be most appropriate for some particular use. All of the games may be run in a short, simplified format or in a more involved and intensive style. For example, AT-ISSUE! is designed with several distinct steps (CROSS-IMPACTING, VARIDENT, and UPPER-LIMIT), any one of which may be used alone or in combination with one of the other games. This flexibility permits adjustment to time constraints as well as to the predilections of the players on any given occasion.

FIGURE I

BASIC CHARACTERISTICS OF THE GAMES

	IMPASSE?	AT ISSUE!	CONCEPTUAL MAPPING...
Intended audience:	Citizen groups, clubs or classes; readers of a book, magazine or newspaper.	Organized citizen groups or classes.	Groups charged with making formal decisions or intensive analysis of a problem.
Purpose:	To inform the player of the complexities associated with an issue; to record opinion; to facilitate discussion.	To obtain the group's prioritization of issues at hand; to assess impact of alternatives; to illustrate cross-impacting of issues.	An operational tool for groups charged with actual decision-making; to structure meetings; to insure continuity of thought between meetings (issues); impact assessment.
Time Required:	Approx. 1 hour.	Approx. 2 hours.	Approx. 4 hours.
Type:	Frame game.	Frame game.	Frame game.
Number of Issues:	One, pre-specified.	A total of 15; any session involves group-determined selection of one.	Unlimited; periodic issue identification process by players.
Typical number of variables:	30 variables.	60 variables.	Approximately 500 variables.
Basic Procedure:	Estimation of impact; review "expert" opinion; discussion.	Selection of issues and statement of values or areas of concern; assessment of impacts on other variables; discussion of conflict between roles.	Selection of issues; assessment of impact on variables; discussion and debate over differences of opinion.
Roles:	One only, 3 players per group.	Multiple roles, 3-5 players per role.	Real-world posture or multiple roles from system (1-3 per role).
Number of Players:	3 upward (optimal 15-35).	15 upward (optimal 15-35).	Up to 15 (optimal 7).
Vote Required on:	Which variables; what impact.	Which issue; which variables; what impact.	Which issue; which variables; impacts.

There are several general characteristics of all three games:

1. Because they are "frame games" they can be readily adapted for a wide range of purposes by those immediately concerned.

2. The basic gaming structure is universal in that it permits virtually any problem to be expressed.

3. Each basic version is thematic - that is, it pertains to one logical problem; many different issues pertaining to the problem can thus be conveniently considered in the same terms.

4. They are parsimonious in that virtually no paraphernalia is required.

5. The length of time of player involvement is flexible and easily controlled; the games can thus be used for short or long-term exercises.

6. Properly selected, the games can be used by small or large groups (3-100) and can be played by individuals or by teams.

7. They may be played in a competitive or cooperative mode.

8. Each version developed can be centrally stored and made available for later use by others, thus providing a library of discussion material.

9. The games lend themselves to mass-media usage either through public distribution (newspapers, magazines) or through organizational distribution (clubs, companies, citizen groups, etc.), in brochure or booklet form (see copyright information on page 49).

10. In the play of these games the player is encouraged to record his/her thoughtful assessment of the impacts of proposed or hypothetical policies; completed game materials can be collected and transmitted to a central source for tabulation and analysis. They can thus be used as questionnaires.

PLAYING IMPASSE?

What is IMPASSE?

IMPASSE? is a simple game presented in a "wheel" or circle broken into 30 pie-shaped sectors (We have constructed IMPASSE? versions with less and with more than 30 sectors, but this number has proved most satisfactory). These sectors contain some set of variables which relate to the problem or event being discussed. The variables are numbered and there is open space in the center for the player to mark an assessment of each variable (see figure II).

A separate "Evaluator" is a small "wheel" or circle which describes the event or policy being considered. The players consider the event or policy in terms of the 30 variables, one by one. In each case a decision about the probable impacts is recorded in the open space. The decisions are made by selecting from a list of five possible choices. When this process is completed, the "Evaluator" wheel is cut out, turned over and placed in the center of the wheel, and the answers of the "expert" are compared with those of the player(s). If players differ with the expert they can turn to the reverse side of the large wheel for a brief explanation of the expert's logic. Players may wish to discuss alternative logical conclusions and thus challenge the "expert."

Remember, the purpose of the game is to stimulate discussion. It should be played by three persons acting as one since their discussions will bring out many facts and tangential arguments. Before playing, groups should be broken into teams of three, and later brought together for large group discussion when assessments and comparisons with the "expert" are completed. The "expert's" logic can be supplemented with an accumulation of facts and reports or even with the "expert" in person.

FIGURE II

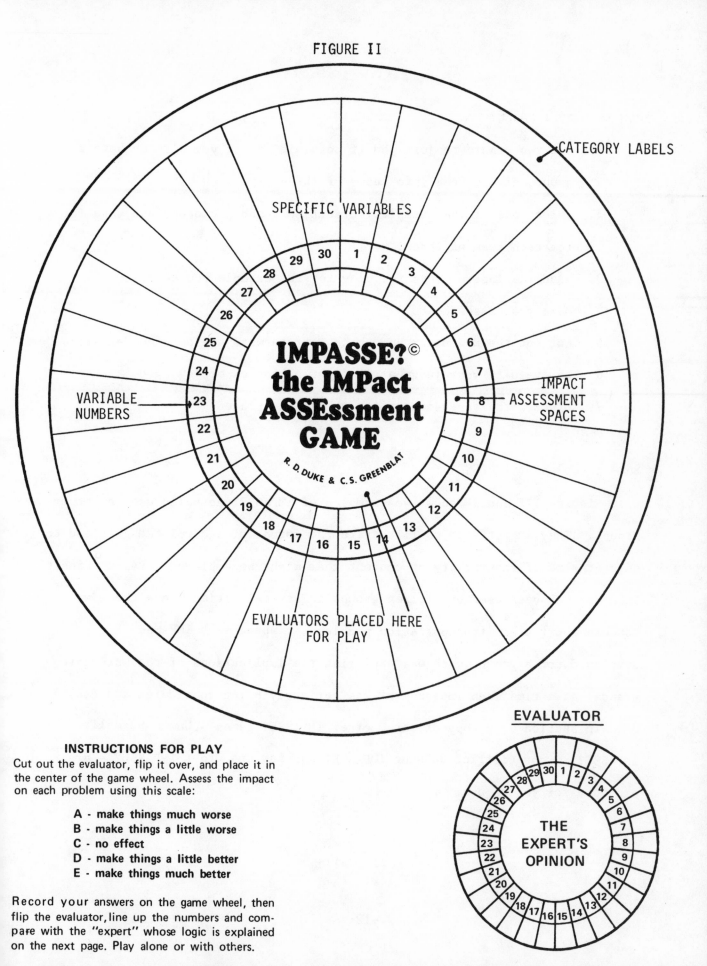

SPECIFIC VARIABLES

CATEGORY LABELS

**IMPASSE?©
the IMPact
ASSEssment
GAME**

R. D. DUKE & C. S. GREENBLAT

VARIABLE NUMBERS

IMPACT ASSESSMENT SPACES

EVALUATORS PLACED HERE FOR PLAY

EVALUATOR

THE EXPERT'S OPINION

INSTRUCTIONS FOR PLAY

Cut out the evaluator, flip it over, and place it in the center of the game wheel. Assess the impact on each problem using this scale:

A - **make things much worse**
B - **make things a little worse**
C - **no effect**
D - **make things a little better**
E - **make things much better**

Record your answers on the game wheel, then flip the evaluator, line up the numbers and compare with the "expert" whose logic is explained on the next page. Play alone or with others.

How to play IMPASSE?

1. Get two others to join you if possible, or if you already have a group, divide them into teams of three.

2. Select one of the examples in section V and photocopy one page for for each team of three.

3. Read the instructions for play for the example you select.

4. Make your assessments.

5. Cut out the Evaluator and check your answers against the "expert's."

6. Re-evaluate your judgment in light of the expert's logic.

7. Discuss the assessments with others who played.

Some examples of IMPASSE?

Figures III and IV show two examples of IMPASSE? actually used by other groups. They are offered to illustrate the format of a completed game and to suggest some of the variety of content that might be employed. Rapid Transit IMPASSE? has been used by citizen groups in several cities where there was concern about urban transportation problems. Impeachment IMPASSE? was developed for a group which was exploring the implications of the Watergate scandal at a time when impeachment was seriously being considered and debated.

In section V, a copy of three other IMPASSE? games - Human Sexuality IMPASSE?, Cross-District Bussing IMPASSE? and Law and Order IMPASSE? - are provided for you to use.

FIGURE III

"RAPID TRANSIT" IMPASSE? ©

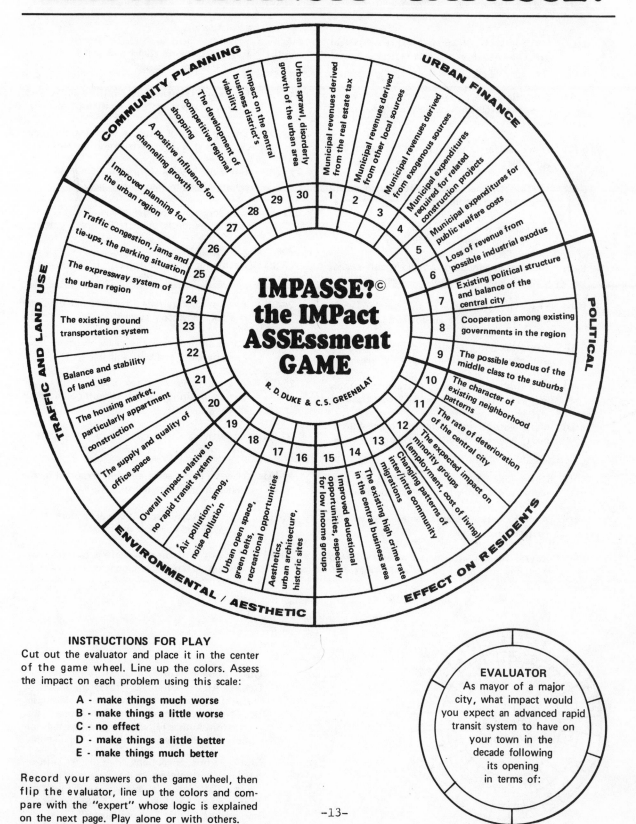

INSTRUCTIONS FOR PLAY

Cut out the evaluator and place it in the center of the game wheel. Line up the colors. Assess the impact on each problem using this scale:

- A - make things much worse
- B - make things a little worse
- C - no effect
- D - make things a little better
- E - make things much better

Record your answers on the game wheel, then flip the evaluator, line up the colors and compare with the "expert" whose logic is explained on the next page. Play alone or with others.

EVALUATOR
As mayor of a major city, what impact would you expect an advanced rapid transit system to have on your town in the decade following its opening in terms of:

-13-

1-(E) Improved viability of the central business district would result in higher land values.

2-(D) More active business climate would result in higher tax derived from business.

3-(E) A successful, advanced rapid transit system will spawn other projects requiring federal aid.

4-(A) Basic changes in transportation capability will result inevitably in secondary costs for roads, sewers, etc.

5-(C) Some welfare recipients will be better off, but others will arrive to replace them.

6-(B) The existing tendancy of industry to decentralize will be encouraged.

7-(B) Populations will shift as land use patterns adjust to transit capability, affecting wards.

8-(E) The very magnitude of a rapid transit system requires discussions; perhaps agreement!

9-(B) The existing tendancy of the middle class to leave the city will be encouraged.

10-(B) Populations will inevitably shift; construction will intrude on existing neighborhoods.

11-(E) A viable rapid transit system inevitably makes a city a more viable "central place".

12-(D) Many actual improvements (low-cost transport, new jobs) will be offset by new indigents.

13-(B) Construction side effects as well as improved mobility will result in shifting populations.

14-(D) A more active, viable central area will discourage street crime.

15-(D) Better transit gives better access, more opportunity to reach a variety of facilities.

16-(B) Construction of this magnitude inevitably causes damage, some of which is permanent.

17-(E) Improved mobility brings a greater area of access to residents; more people moved in a given space.

18-(E) Existing pressures for change will have a better chance for success.

19-(E) No rapid transit system will inevitably lead to more sprawl and deterioration of the city.

20-(D) Entrepreneurial response to a new transport system is dramatic; perhaps too dramatic.

21-(E) The new transport mode will make large areas more accessible to the city.

22-(E) In the long run, more-dense land uses will locate near the terminals; A more European pattern will result.

23-(E) Assuming proper integration (!) more people will commit to public transport.

24-(C) Expressways are here to stay; rapid transport is a complimentary system.

25-(D) Some improvement is to be expected, however the auto is always with us.

26-(D) A rapid transport system is a major component in regional growth permitting improved planning.

27-(E) Growth can be expected to concentrate at the terminals of the rapid transit system.

28-(A) New shopping centers can be expected at the nodes or transit terminals.

29-(E) The central business district will be more readily accessible and therefore more viable.

30-(E) Growth will be channelled by the transit system, planning decisions will be more orderly.

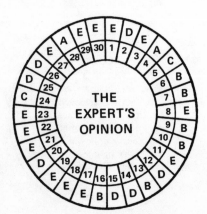

THE EXPERT'S OPINION

Our "expert" for this game is Dr. William Drake, Assoc. Dean for Research, School of Natural Resources, the University of Michigan. Dr. Drake is director of the Ann Arbor Transportation Authority, which has successfully pioneered in the use of "Dial-a-Ride" mini-buses.

Should your perceptions differ (either with regard to the problems in the impasse wheel, the "expert's" values as assessed, or the brief explanation of his choice) drop a note to the editor marked "Rapid Transit Impasse".

Figure IV

★ IMPEACHMENT IMPASSE?ᶜ

David J. Rosen, *Drew University*; Cathy Stein Greenblat, *Rutgers University*; Richard D. Duke, *University of Michigan*

THINKING ABOUT THE IMPACT OF THE POSSIBLE IMPEACHMENT OF PRESIDENT NIXON? Try your hand at assessing the impacts on a series of important dimensions of the current scene. Play alone or better yet, get someone else to play with you. Then compare your assessments with those of an expert: Dr. Steven Salmore of the Eagleton Institute of Politics, Rutgers University.

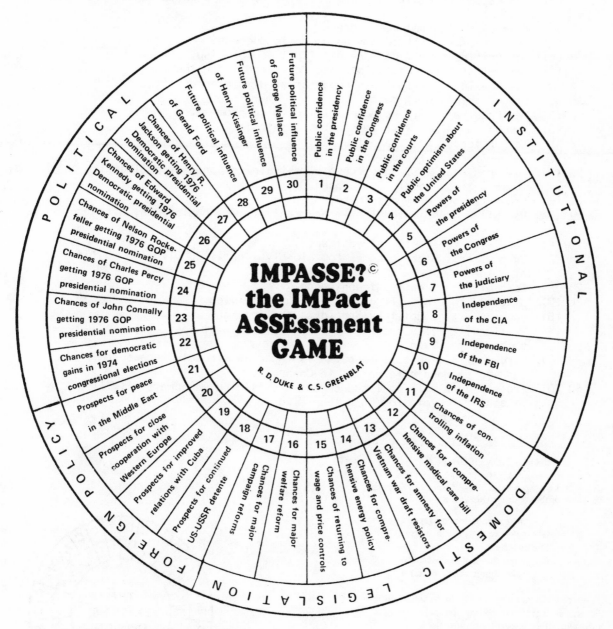

★From: Richard D. Duke and Cathy S. Greenblat, *Game-Generating Games: A Trilogy of Issue-Oriented Games for Community and Classroom.* Environmental Simulation Laboratory, University of Michigan.

THE LOGIC OF THE ASSESSMENTS

1 (A) Public will rally around the new president and he will look good by comparison.
2 (C) Congress may look better to some, but Nixon supporters will be extremely angry.
3 (C) Courts are not directly involved.
4 (A) There will be a perception that a major problem has been overcome.
5 (D) New President will be cautious and more deferential to congress.
6 (B) New President will be cautious and more deferential to congress.
7 (C) Courts are not directly involved.
8 (D) Congress will move to effectively control the CIA for the first time.
9 (B) Increased congressional scrutiny will reduce potential executive control.
10 (C) Already controlled by congress.
11 (C) Other factors will determine economic success.
12 (A) New President will be more willing to compromise.
13 (B) Removal of Nixon would increase "distance" from the war.
14 (B) New President will stress cooperation with congress.
15 (C) Other factors will control.
16 (B) New President will be more willing to compromise.
17 (D) Removal of Nixon will lessen the impetus.
18 (C) Larger forces are operative
19 (C) Larger forces will determine.
20 (D) New President will have trouble restraining Congressional desire to cut troop levels in Europe.
21 (C) Other factors will determine.
22 (B) Republicans who voted for impeachment will be punished by Nixon loyalists.
23 (E) Ford will be greatly strengthened.
24 (E) Unacceptable because he is too closely identified with the ouster of Nixon.
25 (E) Ford will be greatly strengthened.
26 (D) Nixon's troubles will underscore Chappaquidick.
27 (B) Jackson will benefit by Kennedy's decline (see 26).
28 (A) Public will rally around new president who will look very good compared to Nixon.
29 (E) Ford will not be able to back Kissinger as strongly because he will tend to be more deferential to Congress.
30 (D) Protest vote will be lessened and disaffected Democrats will find it easier to vote for Ford than Nixon.

INSTRUCTIONS FOR PLAY

Cut out the evaluator, flip it over, and place it in the center of the game wheel. Assess the impact on each problem using this scale:

A - make things much worse
B - make things a little worse
C - no effect
D - make things a little better
E - make things much better

Record your answers on the game wheel, then flip the evaluator, line up the numbers and compare with the "expert" whose logic is explained on the next page. Play alone or with others.

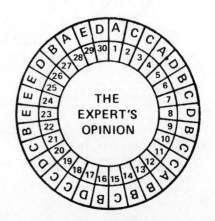

THE EXPERT'S OPINION

Other uses for IMPASSE?

Any problem or context can be added to the blank forms. Some
examples include:

Any community problem (new building, street light, etc.)

An international political question (if country X adopts policy X,
what are the implications for X's relations with 30 nations?).

Natural resource problems (if resource X becomes critically scarce,
what will be the impact on various sectors of the economy?)

A classroom exercise where students are told something such as, "The
readings and lectures have covered a gread deal of material dealing
with X. Consider the following problem which cuts across this material,
and extract the main variables that are relevant for inclusion in an
IMPASSE? wheel. Finally, provide the "expert's" assessment of the
impact of the problem."

Of course, many other potential application exist.

Playing IMPASSE? with your class or group: Style and options.

Impasse? can be used in a variety of styles and circumstances. Some
central thoughts are recorded here. Decisions on play style will affect the
wording of instructions when you build your own version.

A. *Number of Players and Player Organization* - IMPASSE? should normally

(optimally) employ three persons per team, making one joint and

simultaneous decision on each assessment. This maximizes communication

and also permits IMPASSE? to be used for a group of any size by

using a basic unit of three.

Note that large groups, having been divided into teams of three,

can be sectioned into teams dealing with different options (Evaluators).

for example, a group of 45 could first be divided into 15 three-

person sub-groups. Five alternatives could then be considered, three

groups assessing the impact of each. During the critique, discussion

would first be within the three-person subgroups, then between the

five groups of nine persons, each of which considered the different alternatives.

B. *Role Assignment* - The player may be asked to assume a role in assessing impacts. The role will be either:

1. the player's "real-world" (actual) role.

2. some other role, normally that of a public or private decision-maker who can influence the outcome or might be influenced by the outcome of the policy or plan on the Evaluator.

3. the role of some hypothetical person who might influence or be influenced by the policy being gamed (e.g., a potential new position in government; a civil servant; a resident of an area yet to be built).

If the role selection is made explicit, the player obtains more from the experience and the operator and/or evaluator should have a more precise idea of what the recorded decisions imply.

C. *Time* - Players should be limited to a stated time period to complete assessments. The extent of time pressure can be varied by the game operator, but some time pressure should be employed. Approximately one-half hour to do the assessments will usually suffice; at least one-half hour should be allotted for critique.

D. *Fluidity of Play* - Situations occuring during the use of the game should be dealt with quickly and simply (e.g., if a specific variable is not understood, it should be skipped or rewritten and play should continue).

E. *Critique* - A critique must be carefully provided for and should advance through four stages:

1. venting of gripes and/or excitement created by playing the game.

2. specific reactions to the Evaluator(s) by players during the game.

3. discussions between teams who dealt with different options (Evaluators).

4. general discussion as to the players' understanding of the relevance of the experience to its intended real-world counterpart.

Remember that the critique must be focused on the real-world problem under discussion, and that some items of less relevance must be omitted.

F. *Replay* - IMPASSE? readily lends itself to "contemplating the future" or exploring alternative futures in a complex environment. If a group is consistently concerned with a constantly changing future state (e.g., next year's enrollment or staffing; next year's curriculum or market, etc.), the game can be used repeatedly whenever circumstances have changed the perception of what next year might bring.

PLAYING AT-ISSUE!

What is AT-ISSUE!

AT-ISSUE! consists of a series of related activities which can be selectively combined to develop exercises (games) of varying sophistication; thus it can easily be tailored to meet different time constraints. It is similar to IMPASSE? in that a given problem (option, alternative, issue) is evaluated against related variables. It differs in that the participants may select from a list the particular event or issue they want to explore; and a greater level of detail is employed. The basic components in an all-inclusive use of AT-ISSUE! are:

1. A problem description

2. A list of role descriptions

3. Issue-selection cards

4. CROSS-IMPACTING wheel

5. VALUE-ORDERING wheel

6. VARIDENT (variable indentification) wheel

7. Perceived Impact forms

8. UPPER-LIMIT wheel

The game is intended to be played with a group that has some cohesion and the different components may be taken up on several distinct occasions. Time requirements will vary with different steps requiring from 10 or 15 minutes each, or to full consideration of an issue (steps 1-10 below) requiring from 1 to 2 hours to a full evening, depending on the objectives of the user-group and the time they choose to devote to a critique. If the full issue-set is to be played, several meetings will have to be scheduled.

How to play AT-ISSUE!

Details for each step **are** given with each example (**see** section V)
but play goes according to the following steps:

1. *Read the general problem description.*

2. *Role Allocation* - Divide participants into groups- (constituencies,
   usually 3, 5 or 7 per group). If actual members of the constituencies are playing, they can play "themselves" or switch roles. After
   step 3 has been completed, each group should make a brief public
   statement about its concerns.

3. *Value-Ordering* - Each group has a total of 100 value points to allo-
   cate to all the factors on the VALUE-ORDERING wheel (see figure V).
   Allocations must be in multiples of 10's; that is, a factor may be
   assigned a weight of 10, 20, 30, etc., *depending upon how much you
   care about it.* You may spread your points over many factors or
   concentrate on a few; however, the value weights must total 100.
   Indicate whether the factor weighted will have a favorable or unfavor-
   able impact on the issue being gamed. See the instructions on the
   wheel; then fill out the first two columns of the Perceived Impact
   Form (see figure IX) showing which factors you weighted and the amount
   you assigned to each.

4. *Issue Selection* - There are three parts to this step:

   a. Each group sorts the 15 issue cards, selecting the three they
      consider most urgent or most important.

   b. The three issues most frequently selected will be brought to a
      floor vote, with each constituency having 5 votes to allocate as
      they choose. The issue with the highest number of votes will be
      considered first.

-21-

FIGURE V

Group Name _____

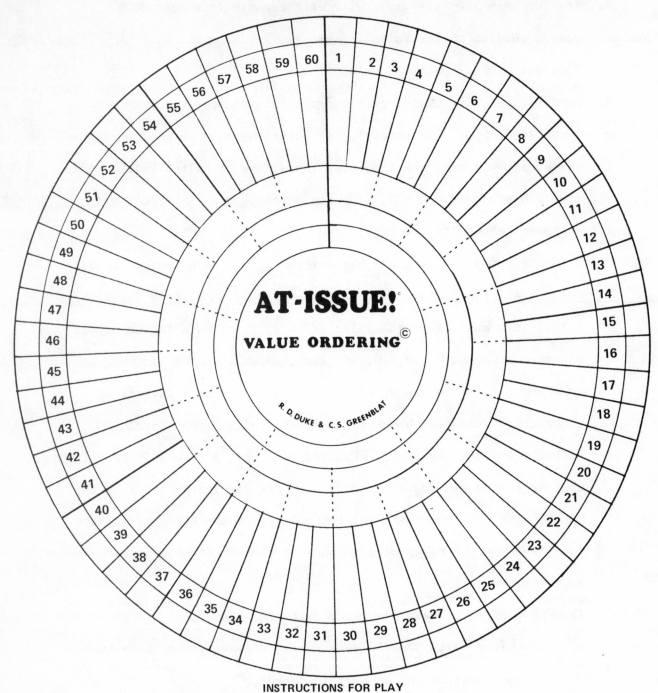

INSTRUCTIONS FOR PLAY

Assign 100 points among the variables, in multiples of 10. These points should indicate the things you most care about. If you would like to see the item increase (e.g., per cent of budget used for schools) put a plus (+) sign in front of your weight. If you would like to see the item decrease (e.g., property tax) put a minus (−) sign in front of the weight

These weights will apply throughout the game so assign them with some care.

c. Decide whether to consider the affirmative or the negative

       resolution of the selected issue, and so mark the issue card.

5. *Cross-Impacting* - Assess the impact of your position on this issue

    upon probable resolution of other issues. Directions are found on

    the CROSS-IMPACTING wheel (see figure VI).

6. *Cross-Group Discussion* - There should now be a short, open discussion

    of the cross-impacting decisions made by the various groups.

7. *Varident* - (variable identification). Assess the impact of your posi-

    tion on each of the factors in the VARIDENT wheel according to the

    directions (see figure VII).

8. *Measure Perceived Impact of the Issue for Your Group* - The impact of

    a position on an issue as felt by your group depends on your assess-

    ments of the impact of the position (step 7) and on how much you care

    about the affected factors (step 3). To obtain a measure of the

    impact as perceived by your group, follow the instructions on the

    Perceived Impact Form (see figure IX). This figure can be compared

    with the figures computed by other groups; it can also be compared

    to similar assessments made by your group on different issues.

9. ****UPPER-LIMIT**** - Add any additional categories that you feel should

    be included on the UPPER-LIMIT wheel (figure VIII). Then follow the

    directions on it.

10. *Critique-Discussion* - Compare and contrast the groups' assessments on

    the VARIDENT wheel and on the Overall Impact Form. Explore similari-

    ties and differences in perceived outcomes; examine concerns over

    outcomes should the position on the issue be adopted.

Repeat this procedure from step 4 for as many issues as you wish to consider.

Value-weights for the factors should remain constant.

FIGURE VI

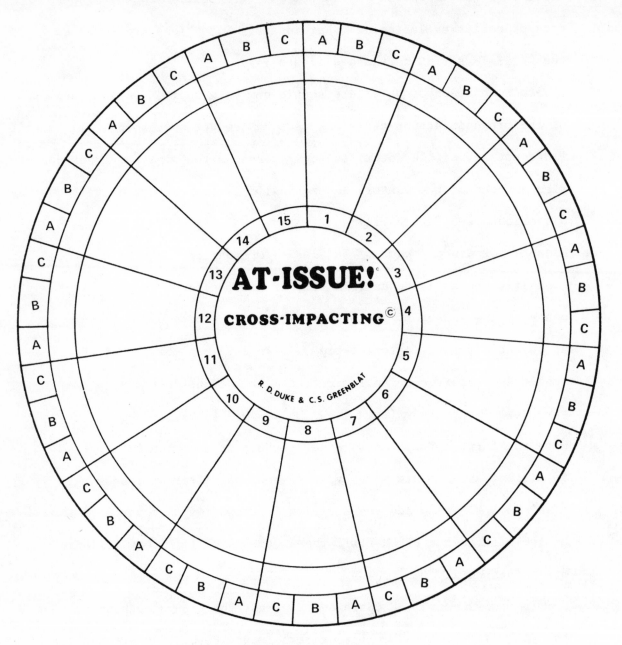

INSTRUCTIONS FOR PLAY

Assess the impact of this issue resolution on all other issues:

A = increased probability of the issue being resolved AFFIRMATIVELY

B = increased probability of the issue being resolved NEGATIVELY

C = NO IMPACT

Issue No. _____   Issue Name _____

_____ Affirmative Resolution   _____ Negative Resolution

Some examples of AT-ISSUE!

There are three examples of AT-ISSUE! presented in section V - Regional Planning AT-ISSUE!; Urban Problems AT-ISSUE!; and Family Dynamics AT-ISSUE! Select the example that is closest to your concerns and play it to see how the game works. If you cannot find enough people to play out the full game at this time, play only one or two of the roles so that you get some understanding of what it entails. This will greatly aid in your understanding of how to build your own version as described in section III.

Other uses for AT-ISSUE!

The examples offered here are only to illustrate the technique. Consider your own needs, and think about how you might recombine these AT-ISSUE! components to help your group. Almost any subject matter can be added to meet your needs.

We have found that many of the components of the Regional Planning version can be employed by people in other areas concerned with issues of Regional Planning. By changing only the role descriptions, issue cards, and CROSS-IMPACTING wheel, for example, the game has been successfully used to deal with problems of development in Manhattan and on Staten Island. You may be able to use components of this or other examples presented here as parts of a new version. If you have time, start with blank materials from section VI and have your group develop their own games.

Playing AT-ISSUE! with your class or group: styles and options

 A. *Number of Players and Player Organization* - AT-ISSUE! can be played
    by groups of varying size, divided into teams (constituencies) of
    from 3 to 7 members. To play, you should identify the groups whose

-25-

FIGURE VII

Group Name _____

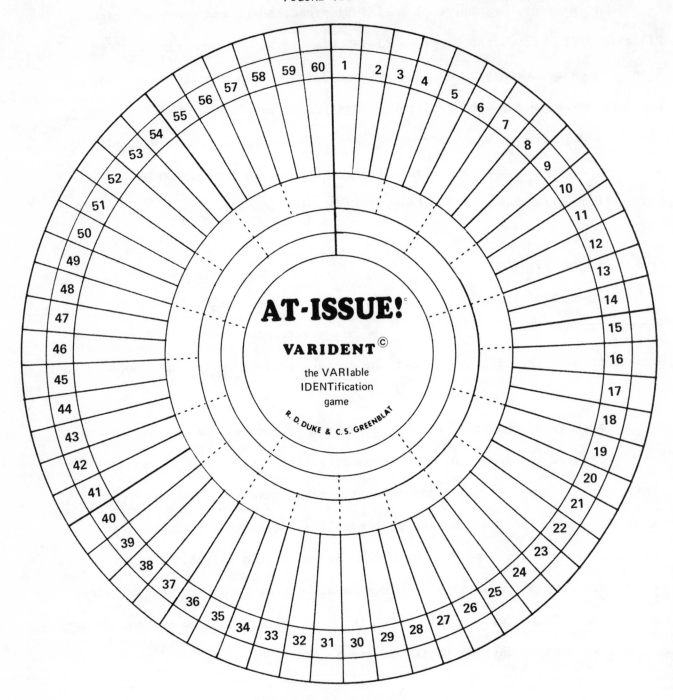

INSTRUCTIONS FOR PLAY

Assess the impact on each variable using this scale:

+2	make things much better
+1	make things a little better
0	no effect
−1	make things a little worse
−2	make things much worse

On the reverse side add any comments you consider appropriate.

perspectives you wish to have represented (e.g., politicians, city planners, residents of area X, etc.) in dealing with the problem. There is no limit to the number that can be identified, but five is often appropriate for smooth play. These can be constituencies in the community or system with a perspective you wish to consider. Players may indicate others they believe should be represented; such additions or substitutions can easily be made.

B. *Role Assignment* - Players should be divided into approximately equal-sized groups (preferably 3, 5, or 7 members each). Each group should assume one of the roles identified in step *A*, above. A player whose real-life role is represented in the game may play his or her own role, or switch.

C. *Time* - Players should be limited to a stated time period for each step. Time allotments will vary depending upon your purpose, the total time available, and the expertise of the players. In general, the following will be a useful time guide:

STEP	*TIME*
1. *Introduce the game and read a general description of the problem.*	*5 minutes*
2. *Role allocation, discussion of the role within the groups, "public statements."*	*15 minutes*
3. *Value-ordering*	*10 minutes*
4. *Issue-selection*	*10 minutes*
5. *Cross-impacting*	*10 minutes*
6. *Cross-group discussion*	*10 minutes*
7. *Varident*	*15 minutes*
8. *Measuring perceived impact*	*10 minutes*
9. *Upper-limit*	*10 minutes*
10. *Critique-Discussion*	*25 minutes*

Total: *2 hours*
Total iterative steps (4-10):   *1 1/2 hours*

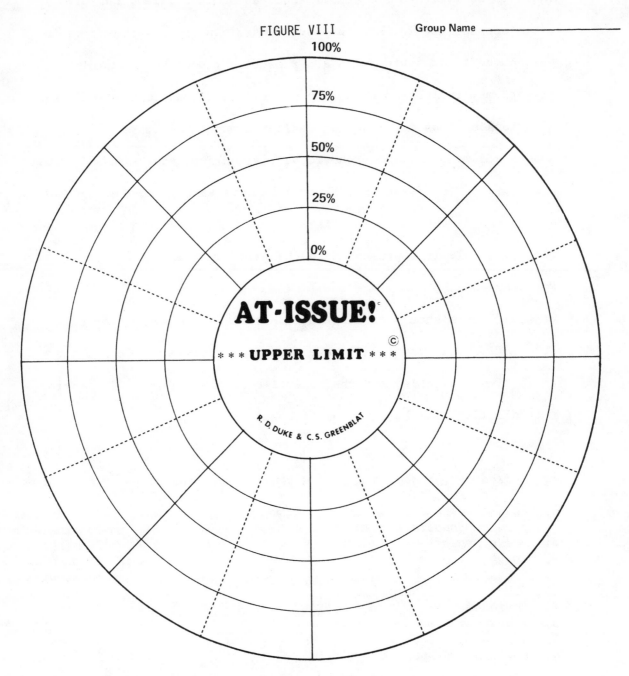

FIGURE VIII

Group Name _____

100%

75%

50%

25%

0%

AT-ISSUE!

* * * **UPPER LIMIT** * * *

R. D. DUKE & C. S. GREENBLAT

INSTRUCTIONS FOR PLAY

1. Mark each variable to indicate the current level of use (to what extent is the system already burdened?). Connect all marks to form a circle.

2. Repeat with a different colored pencil, BUT mark each variable as you expect it to be five years from now, based on the stated resolution of the issue under discussion.

D. *Fluidity of Play* – Situations occurring during the use of the game should be dealt with quickly and simply; for example, if a specific variable is not understood, it should be skipped or rewritten and play should continue.

E. *Critique* – The critique-discussion should be fairly informal but should allow for several types of questions and comments:

1. venting of gripes and/or excitement created by playing the game.

2. specific reactions to the policy or issue considered.

3. comparison between groups of assessments, values, and perceived impacts.

4. general sense of the relevance of the experience to its intended real-world counterpart. The critique must be focused on the real-world problem under discussion, and thus some items of less relevance must be omitted when time is limited.

Figure IX

AT-ISSUE! Perceived Impact Form

Group_____

Issue #_____

Position: affirmative resolution_____ negative resolution _____

Factor Number	Value Weight (10, 20...)	X	Impact (from VARIDENT) (+2,+1,0,-1,-2)	=	Perceived Impact
_____	_____	X	_____	=	_____
_____	_____	X	_____	=	_____
_____	_____	X	_____	=	_____
_____	_____	X	_____	=	_____
_____	_____	X	_____	=	_____
_____	_____	X	_____	=	_____
_____	_____	X	_____	=	_____
_____	_____	X	_____	=	_____
_____	_____	X	_____	=	_____
_____	_____	X	_____	=	_____
_____	_____	X	_____	=	_____
_____	_____	X	_____	=	_____
_____	_____	X	_____	=	_____
_____	_____	X	_____	=	_____
_____	_____	X	_____	=	_____
_____	_____	X	_____	=	_____
_____	_____	X	_____	=	_____
_____	_____	X	_____	=	_____
_____	_____	X	_____	=	_____

Your group's total perceived impact on this issue   = _____

Directions: Enter the factor number and the value weight for all factors you assigned a weight of more than 0. Enter the impacts you assessed for these factors in the VARIDENT procedure. Multiply each of these and add the Perceived Impact column.

PLAYING THE CONCEPTUAL MAPPING GAME...

What is the CONCEPTUAL MAPPING GAME...

The **CONCEPTUAL MAPPING GAME**... differs from both of the exercises previously described. Its purpose, of course, is basically the same - to help a group organize a productive discussion about a complex issue. The style mimics the previous two games; and, although the level of complexity is much greater (variables numbering in the hundreds rather than in the tens), the procedures for use are more simple.

The prime purpose of the CONCEPTUAL MAPPING GAME... is to provide a visual check-list against which a specific problem can be considered. It is assumed that the group using the CONCEPTUAL MAPPING GAME... is somewhat smaller in size (3-15 people) than the groups that can be accomodated with the first two games. It is also assumed that the players are knowledgeable about the problem, or are seriously interested in becoming so.

The CONCEPTUAL MAPPING GAME... might more appropriately be called a game-like exercise. Its purpose is to encourage a group with a shared concern or problem to give more systematic thought to the complexity of that problem, and to provide a vehicle to that end. In playing the game (or participating in the exercise) players can view a variety of possible futures by viewing the effects on a series of variables of a specific resolution of the issue confronting them. The cumulative effects of a number of resolutions on any *particular* variable can also be seen.

The value of the game is not to be found solely in the documentation obtained, although this may be of considerable utility. Rather, the value is vested in the increasingly accurate and enlarged perception of the problem by those wrestling with it. The procedure is particularly effective in providing new members to the group with a sense of the thought that preceded their entry.

The procedure demands fresh evaluations from older members as they discover the kaleidoscopic interactions resulting from the alternative resolution of a series of issues.

There are two stages in the use of the CONCEPTUAL MAPPING GAME...: (1) play of a priming game – a simple introduction with IMPASSE? or the VARIDENT wheel from AT-ISSUE!; and (2) play of the CONCEPTUAL MAPPING GAME...itself.

How to play the CONCEPTUAL MAPPING GAME...

There are several ways to use the game, but the following is the procedure we recommend for the first introductory play period:

1. If possible, play an IMPASSE? game before attempting this game. It serves as a good introduction. If time permits, playing AT-ISSUE! will also be helpful, but it is not a necessary step.

2. Have a discussion of the problem, and post a written statement for easy reference and modification as play progresses.

3. Have each individual select a role (possibly the person's real-world role); alternatively, if the group is large, have three people work as a single role.

4. Select the particular issue to be dealt with at this time.

5. As a team effort, identify the variables on the CONCEPTUAL MAPPING wheel (section VI) which would be affected by the issue under discussion. For each variable affected, indicate with a flow pen on the wheel the appropriate number from the following scale:

   +2 strong positive impact on this variable

   +1 some positive impact on this variable

    0 impact unknown

    -1 some negative impact on this variable

    -2 severe negative impact on this variable

An alternative to using the numbers is to use colored flow pens to outline the variable cell (do not color in the entire cell as it will obscure the print). This may make the final wheel more legible from a distance if the colors are carefully chosen and care is used when outlining the cells.

Some examples of the CONCEPTUAL MAPPING GAME...

Three examples are included in section V for your use - Regional Planning CONCEPTUAL MAPPING GAME; Criminal Justice System CONCEPTUAL MAPPING GAME; and the Public School System CONCEPTUAL MAPPING GAME. Select the game that most interests you and follow the instructions for play as given above.

Other uses of the CONCEPTUAL MAPPING GAME...

The CONCEPTUAL MAPPING GAME...has proven useful in a wide variety of circumstances characterized by sophisticated discussion of important and complex issues by senior people in both research and decision-making. In addition to the use in Monterey Bay described in section I, the game has been used:

> by senior civil servants in the Netherlands meeting to consider alternative schemes for a major airport relocation;

> by local officials, industry representatives, government officials and research people in Manitoba, Canada concerned with problems brought about by oil exploration in the Hudson Bay lowlands area;

> by a team of engineers preparing a major study on geothermal energy development who used the game to develop the outline for a summary report to be presented to the U.S. Congress.

There have been a wide variety of additional uses. This framework is suitable for any subject matter if time and circumstances warrant a high level of effort. The conceptual rationale for this approach is presented in detail in GAMING: THE FUTURE'S LANGUAGE, by Richard D. Duke, Halstead Press, 1974.

Playing the CONCEPTUAL MAPPING GAME... with your class or group: styles and options.

A. *Elaboration of the Procedure for Playing with a Larger Group* - There are two procedural routes that can be followed in employment of CONCEPTUAL MAPPING GAME... In the basic version, the wheel and issues are prepared in advance by the game director or a designated sub-group. In the elaborate version, these game elements are initially prepared by the group. In either case, the following steps pertain. They represent an elaboration of the steps recommended for the first introductory play of the game.

1. Provide a conceptual map indicating the variables pertinent to the general problem at hand (e.g., regional planning for the Monterey Bay area) and a list of issues known or suspected to exist, or a list of policies to be considered.

2. Introduce the gaming procedure briefly, and explain the general problem.

3. Have the group members prioritize the issues so as to select the (first) issue to be considered. This can be done most easily in the following way:

   a. Ask each member to sort the issues into those of high, medium and low concern to him or her.

   b. Select the five issues receiving the highest number of votes; tell players they will be able to cast three votes to select the one issue to be considered. All three votes can be cast on the same issue or the votes can be divided; this allows players to weight issues.

   c. Allow time for discussion and bargaining.

d. Take votes and announce the issue to be considered.

4. Divide the total group into subgroups of either 3, 5 or 7 members.

5. Cut a copy of the CONCEPTUAL MAP into sectors and distribute one sector to each small group.

   An alternative method that has been successfully employed is to assign 3-5 persons to each complete wheel. From the perspective of a given role and correlated scenario, they systematically examine all the variables on the wheel in response to this question, "If ____ happens, what will the impact be on variable ____?" Their decisions are recorded directly on the wheel with colored flow pens (e.g., red - makes things worse; yellow - no effect; green - makes things better). Simultaneously, other groups are examining other conceptual mapping wheels, using the same question, but different roles/scenarios. When all groups are finished, the wheels are posted and a joint critique is held.

6. Announce a scoring procedure (e.g., the numbering system indicated previously or a color key) and a time period for all groups to consider the impacts of the issue resolutions on the variables in their sector of the wheel. Time for this process will vary according to the number of variables in the wheel and sectors, the complexity of the problem, the sophistication of the group and the total time available.

7. When all the assessments have been completed, initiate the summary/ review session. Each group should select a spokesperson. One by one the spokespeople should present the group consensus on the direction and magnitude of effect on any variable in their sector

believed to be affected by the issue/policy. A staff member or the operator should record these on a fresh copy of the wheel, resorting to group vote if necessary, and noting any major controversies.

8. If a number of issues are to be considered, a master wheel can be prepared which contains a record of the direction of the impacts of several of the issues.

The procedure is iterative; any number of issues can be considered by starting again from step three with a new cut-up copy of the map and a new copy for the summary.

B. *Number of Players and Player Organization* - The CONCEPTUAL MAPPING GAME... can be used with 3 to 15 players; simultaneous runs permit any size group to be accomodated. In general, one master and one cut-up wheel per issue should be used with up to 15 players. When there are more than this number, it is wise to divide into sub-games of 15 each, with each having a "recorder" following the procedures outlined above.

C. *Role Assignment* - The same instructions pertain here as for IMPASSE?; that is, the player may be asked to assume a "role" in assessing impacts. The role will be either:

1. the player's "real-world" (actual) role.

2. some other role, normally that of a public or private decision-maker who can influence the outcome or might be influenced by the outcome of the policy or plan under consideration.

3. the role of some hypothetical person who might influence or be influenced by the policy being gamed (e.g., a potential new position in government; a civil servant; a resident of a new area

yet to be built).

If the role selection is made explicit, the player obtains more from the experience and the operator and/or evaluator should have a more precise idea of what the recorded decisions imply.

D. *Time* - A minimum of four hours is required for play, to be followed by discussion/critique. Approximately 1/2 hour is required for each small group to familiarize itself with the role and the question or scenario. About three hours should be used for assigning the color-coded or scaled-number responses to the wheel. Finally, the group indicates what they see to be the relative importance of the variable marked.

E. *Fluidity of Play* - Problems arising during the play of the game should be dealt with quickly and simply (e.g., if a specific variable is not understood, it should be skipped or rewritten and play should continue).

F. *Critique* - A critique should follow the same steps indicated earlier in discussing the critique for IMPASSE? However, a separate time period should be reserved for the purpose. Each group should have an opportunity to describe their reaction to the assigned role/scenario that they played (about 5-10 minutes per group) and then an unstructured discussion should be encouraged of about two hours duration.

G. *Using the Results* - When a group of some sophistication has completed the play of the CONCEPTUAL MAPPING GAME... the master summary wheel represents an elaborate record of the anticipated impacts of an issue resolution. This can readily be used to "load" an IMPASSE? game and to provide "expert's" opinions so that others less knowledgable about the problem can learn from the results of play of the more elaborate game.

III. MAKE YOUR OWN GAMES

BUILDING IMPASSE?

Components to be prepared.

A completed IMPASSE? game consists of several elements, listed below. Some elements (marked with an *) need not be written, but the group leader or operator must decide upon them and report to the players. You must, then, prepare the following:

*1. A statement which presents a substantive overview of the problem, situation or issue being gamed. This serves as an introduction and background; it should be brief and factual (normally less than 2,500 words), and may contain text or graphics, as appropriate.

*2. A brief description of the game.

*3. A statement of *purpose* or *objective* for the particular exercise, including the substantive circumstances for its use, expected *time requirements*, and characteristics of the *intended audience* (probable age ranges, number of players, etc.). This should be less than 500 words.

*4. Critique procedures describing the time allocation, objectives and mechanisms for insuring public discussion (less than 250 words).

*5. A version of the IMPASSE? wheel containing concentric circles for (outer circle to inner circle):

- category labels

- descriptive variables

- numbering of variables

- impact assessment recording spaces (single or multiple)

- game title; this space also serves as the location for the Evaluator (small wheel) during play.

-38-

When completed, the categories may be color-coded (see figure II).

6. A set of instructions for play, including the assessment scale to be used.

7. The Evaluators. The Evaluator is a small wheel, on one side of which will be written a policy, question, event, proposal or solution that might affect the variables or be affected by them. Around the perimeter on the flip side of the Evaluator are segments corresponding to the variable segments in the IMPASSE? wheel. The "expert's assessments" or "answers" are recorded in the segments, using the same assessment scale used by the players. This side of the Evaluator could be color-coded or otherwise keyed to the wheel category to facilitate lining it up when it is placed on the IMPASSE? wheel.

8. The arguments behind the experts' opinion should be briefly stated in writing; normally one sentence for each recorded "expert opinion" will suffice.

Basic procedures for designing a version of IMPASSE?

There are blank IMPASSE? forms in section VI. To load content in the IMPASSE? frame, you must do the following:

1. *Select the Categories and the Descriptive Variables* - Using the overview of the problem and the statement of purpose prepared earlier, identify both the *major categories* of variables affecting the problem and the *variables*. The division of the problem (or issue) into major categories and descriptive variables might be suggested by the substance or logic of the problem being gamed; or it might be based on the importance of the variables to the players (the latter option would require a preliminary exercise in which the players evaluated

the priorities of potential items for the variable set). Divide
each category in such a fashion that you generate multiple descriptive
variables (30 seems appropriate, and there are 30 spaces on the blank
IMPASSE? forms, but the number that can be employed may vary
The descriptive variables must all be related to the central issue; mixing
irrelevant variables into a game only serves to confuse the players.
The most common types of descriptive variables that can be employed are
included in the following list:

a. A logical problem-set, presenting sets of variables integral to an
   issue (e.g., political problems, revenue raising problems, etc.).

b. Budget items which in total define the major sources of revenue or
   items of expenditure in a system).

c. Geographical units composing a logical set (e.g., census tracts,
   political wards, school districts).

d. Any organizational set, whether or not of an hierarchical nature.

Fill these in on the wheel, and if you wish, color-code or shade the
major categories on both the wheel and the Evaluator(s).

2. *Make the Evaluator(s) to Be Used with Your Variable Set* - Make as many
   as are necessary to express all aspects of the issue under consideration
   by entering proposals, plans, etc,, on blank Evaluator forms. The
   Evaluator can contain one logical statement or issue, real or hypothetical, which will be engaged with the large wheel items. The Evaluator statement must be closely and logically linked to the variable set
   employed, and it must be both intelligible and important to the intended
   audience. Use of vernacular in both elements will help to insure that
   the exercise is relevant for the anticipated audience. In most cases,

-40-

the Evaluator statement should be action-specific - a tangible, possible, feasible act or policy influencing the variables. It will frequently be one of the following types:

a. Any *policy* - public or private, administrative or legal, past, present or speculative - related to the variable set employed in the IMPASSE? wheel.

b. Any *course of action* - actual or hypothetical, related to the variable set employed.

c. Any *event* - planned, accidental or routine - logically related to the variable set employed.

d. Any *issue* about which discussion is sought.

e. Any *specific variable* from the set employed in the IMPASSE? wheel. Terminology for both the Evaluators and the large wheel should be consistently and precisely employed. The designer must select one of two modes:

a. An attempt at concise, value-free terminology (e.g., "Solid Waste Disposal" rather than "Garbage Overflow Problem"). This is highly recommended, because it requires the players to define the meaning of the terms employed.

b. Value-loaded terminology which is integral to a particular public agency (e.g., "Improved Public Transportation" euphemizing for the more accurate "Build More Freeways"). If value-loaded terminology is employed, players must be told who prepared the materials and their basic posture on the topic at hand.

3. *Define the Assessment Scale to Be Used* - This will typically be one of the following:

a. Make it (them) much better

b. Make it (them) a little better

c. No effect

d. Make it (them) a little worse

e. Make it (them) much worse

or

a. Increase it (them) greatly

b. Increase it (them) a little

c. No effect

d. Decrease it (them) a little

e. Decrease it (them) greatly

4. *Provide the "Expert's Assessment" of the Impact of the Evaluator(s).*
   This should take two forms:

   a. The impact as estimated by the experts must be recorded on the reverse side of the Evaluator using the assessment scale given to the players.

   b. The logic for this evaluation should be written in brief form and distributed to the players prior to discussion. You may wish to have an "expert" in the field play your game and provide the assessment which will be given to subsequent players, or you may write the assessment yourself.

5. *Prepare a Sufficient Number of Copies for Your Group to Use.*

BUILDING AT-ISSUE!

Components to be prepared.

As was true for IMPASSE?, play style will affect the wording in the design process. AT-ISSUE! was designed for groups that meet regularly for periods of two to four hours. The materials can be prepared in advance; or can be "loaded" with content while the group is present; or members of the group can prepare the materials as "homework" between meeting dates.

AT-ISSUE! is made up in units or component exercises that can be combined in different patterns. Large groups can run parallel exercises. This introduces an element of competition and facilitates discussion during the critique. This dual flexibility of modular construction and the possibility of simultaneous, parallel exercises allows the user to meet the needs of groups of varying characteristics.

AT-ISSUE! has eight distinct components:

1. *Problem Description* - This should be brief and factual, normally two typed pages.

2. *List of the Role Descriptions* - These should define each role to be employed in terms of major decisions made and logical links to other roles.

3. *Issue-Selection Cards* - These are 4" x 5" cards which briefly describe issues of interest to the group. Their purpose is to permit a range of problems to be raised for possible consideration and to provide a vehicle for issue-selection for further study.

4. *Cross-Impacting Wheel* - This permits the players to consider the impact of their selection of a given issue on other, related issues. Its objective is to provide an overview before getting deeply involved in a problem.

5. *Value-Ordering Wheel* - This allows each group of players to select variables of special concern. It requires that they assign a value to variables which reflect their degree of interest.

6. *VARIDENT (Variable Identification) Wheel* - This lets each group of players make a judgement about the nature and extent of impact an issue will have on the variables.

7. *Perceived Impact Form* - This is a scorecard which lets each team evaluate the perceived impact of an issue, based on their own values and their own judgment of impacts. This scoring device is very helpful during the critique period in determining different reasoning from team to team (role to role).

8. *UPPER-LIMIT Wheel* - This requires the players to extract a few of the most critical variables, and to make a judgement as to how they will be affected through time by the issue in question.

Basic procedures for designing a version of AT-ISSUE!

Blank copies of all forms are provided in section VI. Because AT-ISSUE! can be used in many different combinations, each user will have to use some imagination in determining the procedure for his/her purpose. Several major steps are involved:

1. Analyze your audience. What is its size? Purpose? Age configuration? How much time do they have for each meeting? How often do they meet?

2. Decide whether to prepare a full set of completed forms or to have group members prepare the forms (the latter option should not be employed with a group that has not played a "priming" version of AT-ISSUE!; either prepare your own example or use one included in this volume). The remaining steps should be undertaken by you or the group

as a whole. The suggestions covering terminology, etc. offered in the section on building IMPASSE? are also relevant here.

3. Prepare a written problem statement which is brief and factual. Assemble any reports or other data that address the issue, and keep them on hand for the players to use. The problem statement should give an overview of the topic or issue. It should list as many issues as possible that might be pending. The report should also identify the major interest groups (i.e., game roles) and decisions involved. If possible, information should be prepared about these various constituencies and their concerns in the form of a list of brief role descriptions.

4. The data gathered during step three (above) should be reviewed for a list of variables to be included in the VALUE-ORDERING AND VARIDENT wheels. These variables can be prepared as lists to offer to the players for their use in preparing these two basic wheels; or, it may be preferable to place the variables on the wheels to permit the players to immediately begin issue evaluation. If this option is followed, be sure to leave enough blank space for the players to add variables that might be forgotten. Follow the instructions in the section on building versions of IMPASSE?

5. Review the information gathered during step three for the most critical variables for inclusion in the UPPER-LIMIT wheel. These should be factors which are most seriously affected by the issues under investigation.

6. Reproduce a sufficient number of copies of each form for your group.

BUILDING THE CONCEPTUAL MAPPING GAME...

Components to be prepared.

The CONCEPTUAL MAPPING GAME... **has three** primary objectives: to convey a gestalt or overview of a complex situation; to present very detailed ideas in the context of this overview; and to illustrate, visually, the linkages which emerge between the various components. The basic frame game has been formulated to permit the presentation of an involved problem at whatever level of abstraction is appropriate to the user group.

The CONCEPTUAL MAPPING GAME... consists of minimal materials:

1. A "wheel" or conceptual map in the format of a series of concentric circles divided into sectors and sub-sectors. Each sector contains a major topical variable-set. The most general categories are in the innermost circles, and greater levels of detail are indicated from the center out. Two techniques of mapping can be used:

   a. Make two paper "maps" per issue considered - one that is cut up and divided among players, and one for recording the summary effects.

   b. Make a "master wheel," possibly mounted, marked with pins or stickers to indicate cumulative effects of the *series* of issues considered. This bears a rough relationship to the type of display map found in a police station showing crimes or accidents at particular locations.

2. A statement of the general problem (e.g., regional planning).

3. A list of issues and alternative solutions presently facing the group or expected to emerge in the future.

4. A description of a scoring or impacting procedure which will be used to indicate the relationship between an issue and the variables on the Conceptual Map. The procedure entails selecting the variables affected,

noting the direction of the effect, and indicating the magnitude of the effect. Scoring, as noted earlier, can be done with numbers (positive and negative) or with a color key.

5. Instructions to the operator concerning the review and modification procedure. This allows for alteration of the basic wheel, summary and review of the effects of the issue gamed, and consideration of those effects in the context of other issues.

Basic procedures for designing a CONCEPTUAL MAPPING GAME...

1. The procedures described in the sections on building IMPASSE? and AT-ISSUE! games will explain how to construct all the components of a CONCEPTUAL MAPPING GAME... except the large map.

2. To create the map is a rather lengthy process, but it is really an elaboration of the processes you have used in creating the simpler games. In an orderly way, accumulate data, bits of theory, descriptions, linkages, role descriptions and other pieces of information that seem relevant to the issue. Collect these without undue concern for their coherence; do not make an initial evaluation as to their probable final utility. Each of these assembled ideas or problem descriptors is now to be placed on separate 3" x 5" cards, with a brief description. A descriptive heading should be at the top of each card.

You may wish to work from here with the cards themselves, or you may find it easier to transfer the headings to small slips of paper, each including only the variable name, for example:

| plant size | | water supply | | detection |

On some appropriate space, preferably a large wall with a tack board surface, the clusters of headings should now be arranged in a temporary fashion, group by group, as appropriate. When any heading seems to be out of place, or to fit relatively well into two or more places, you should discuss the best location. In the initial process, the clusters will be quite small, consisting of only three to five descriptors logically related. Gradually, the clusters will become larger and will include logical subgroupings.

In the next phase, the display area is organized into a wheel into which all of the clusters must be inserted. This will eliminate some ideas of lesser significance and will inevitably cause the discovery of gaps which must be filled in. As individual clusters are correlated and formed into sectors of the wheel, an argument must develop as to the appropriateness of a variable set vis-a-vis the entire picture.

The process described is iterative, and should continue until the group performing the task is satisfied that the wheel is an accurate abstraction of their perception of reality.

IV. GETTING YOUR GAME INTO USE

SUGGESTIONS AND COPYRIGHT RESTRICTIONS

When you have successfully developed your own game, you will face two problems - getting the materials copied for your own use and giving your version of the game wider circulation among those who might be interested.

The technology for inexpensive reproduction of materials changes locally, but the best option for small quantities (under 50) is to use a commercial copy machine that gives two-sided copy. If the quantity required exceeds 50, it may be best to have a local printing shop make the copies on an offset press.

If you complete a version that works well, and would like it to be made available to a larger audience, mail it to us at RADIUS INTERNATIONAL, 321 Parklake, Ann Arbor, Michigan, 48103. We hope to select the best materials available and publish these as examples to help new groups to get started. Be sure to include your name and address and the citation you would like to see on the published version. Use the printed forms in the back of the book. We will contact you as soon as possible upon receipt of the materials.

IMPASSE?, AT-ISSUE! and the CONCEPTUAL MAPPING GAME... are fully protected by the Federal Copyright Act, Patent Act and Trademark Act. The procedures and circumstances governing the use of these materials are as follows:

1. Copies of existing versions of the game themes and options may be used for non-profit and/or public purposes if the materials are secured from authorized published sources or if independent written agreements for use have been established with the authors or an assigned agent. All existing versions of the games must retain all copyright, patent and trademark statements in the center, as shown; titles of new versions and names of designers of new versions should be at the top

of the page.

2. New and/or innovative variations of the games (either new versions or new materials employed with existing versions), and mechanical changes dealing with use and/or evaluation are encouraged. However, they must be approved in writing prior to publication or use by the innovator for any non-profit purpose. Written agreements are necessary if a profit-oriented use in envisioned. In both instances, uninhibited rights of publication of the new material will be transferred to the original game designers. All new versions of the games must retain all copyright, patent and trademark statements in the Center, as shown; Titles of new versions and names of designers of new versions should be at the top of the page.

3. Periodically, as circumstances may warrant, the original designers intend to publish, for private, public or commercial distribution, selected examples of the games and information concerning circumstances of their use.

GET YOUR GAME PUBLISHED!

Please type or print!

Your Name_____ Phone No._____

                                                                      (area code)(number)

Address_____

City_____

State_____ Zip_____

Title of your game_____
_____

Citation as you would like it to appear, if printed:_____
_____
_____
_____

What institution or organization was the game prepared for?_____
_____
_____

Why did you build the game?_____
_____
_____
_____

Attach your game and sign this form to authorize us to publish your example. We will then contact you.

Date_____   _____
                                     Signature

Please mail to RADIUS INTERNATIONAL, 321 Parklake, Ann Arbor, Michigan, 48103.

V. EXAMPLES FOR PLAY

IMPASSE? EXAMPLES

Overview.

There are three IMPASSE? games presented here for you to play. A copy of each is included. More elaborate instructions for play than those included here are in section II of this manual. The examples are:

1. HUMAN SEXUALITY IMPASSE? by Cathy S. Greenblat and John Gagnon. This version was designed for and included in John H. Gagnon and Bruce Henderson, HUMAN SEXUALITY. Little, Brown and Company, Inc., 1975.

2. LAW AND ORDER IMPASSE? by Richard D. Duke and Barbara Goldberg. This version was created as an example for this manual.

3. CROSS-DISTRICT SCHOOL BUSSING IMPASSE? by Richard D. Duke and Barbara Goldberg. This is a new version created as an example for this manual.

HUMAN SEXUALITY IMPASSE?

Cathy Greenblat
John Gagnon

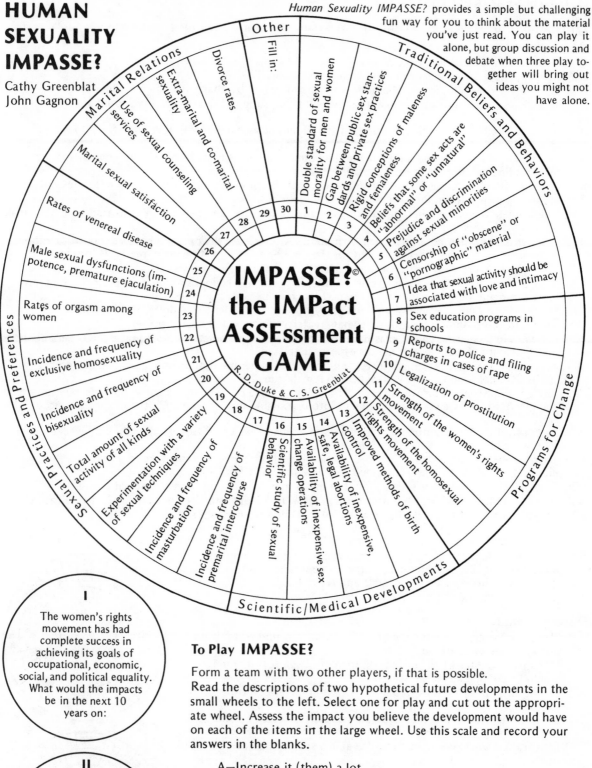

Human Sexuality IMPASSE? provides a simple but challenging fun way for you to think about the material you've just read. You can play it alone, but group discussion and debate when three play together will bring out ideas you might not have alone.

IMPASSE?©
the IMPact
ASSEssment
GAME

R. D. Duke & C. S. Greenblat

Items in the large wheel (reading around):

Other — Fill in: — 28 — 29 — 30
Traditional Beliefs and Behaviors:
1. Double standard of sexual morality for men and women
2. Gap between public sex standards and private sex practices
3. Rigid conceptions of maleness and femaleness
4. Beliefs that some sex acts are "abnormal" or "unnatural"
5. Prejudice and discrimination against sexual minorities
6. Censorship of "obscene" or "pornographic" material
7. Idea that sexual activity should be associated with love and intimacy
8. Sex education programs in schools
9. Reports to police and filing charges in cases of rape
10. Legalization of prostitution

Programs for Change:
11. Strength of the women's rights movement
12. Strength of the homosexual rights movement
13. Improved methods of birth control
14. Availability of inexpensive, safe, legal abortions
15. Availability of inexpensive sex change operations

Scientific/Medical Developments:
16. Scientific study of sexual behavior
17. Incidence and frequency of premarital intercourse
18. Incidence and frequency of masturbation
19. Experimentation with a variety of sexual techniques

Sexual Practices and Preferences:
20. Total amount of sexual activity of all kinds
21. Incidence and frequency of bisexuality
22. Incidence and frequency of exclusive homosexuality
23. Rates of orgasm among women
24. Male sexual dysfunctions (impotence, premature ejaculation)
25. Rates of venereal disease

Marital Relations:
26. Marital sexual satisfaction
27. Use of sexual counseling services
28. Extra-marital and co-marital sexuality
29. Divorce rates

I

The women's rights movement has had complete success in achieving its goals of occupational, economic, social, and political equality. What would the impacts be in the next 10 years on:

II

All public depictions or exposures of the human body (male and female) in any degree of nudity from the neck to the knee have been declared obscene and illegal by the Supreme Court, with severe penalties for offenders. What would the impact be in the next 10 years on:

To Play IMPASSE?

Form a team with two other players, if that is possible.

Read the descriptions of two hypothetical future developments in the small wheels to the left. Select one for play and cut out the appropriate wheel. Assess the impact you believe the development would have on each of the items in the large wheel. Use this scale and record your answers in the blanks.

A—Increase it (them) a lot
B—Increase it (them) a little
C—No effect
D—Decrease it (them) a little
E—Decrease it (them) a lot

Then flip the small wheel over and compare your answers with those of the expert, John Gagnon. On the other side of this flap are explanations for his answers.

From R.D. Duke and C.S. Greenblat, *Game-Generating Games.* Boston: Little, Brown and Company, in preparation.

HUMAN SEXUALITY IMPASSE?

Explanations for The Expert's Opinion (Where no exlanation is given, the expert's opinion was "no effect").

Development I

E 1. General political-economic inequality is part of the basis of sexual inequality.

E 3. Beliefs in necessary gender roles will largely disappear.

D 4. Acceptance of variety in sexual practices will be increased by changed women's roles.

D 5. The success of a major social equality movement that supports sexual equality should aid sexual minorities.

B 7. The commonly held female position that sex should be associated with love and affection will gain strength.

A 9. Changes in women's rights should make the police and courts more responsive to women and women more willing to report male sex agression.

A10. Occupational freedom is one of the main points of the women's movement; while not necessarily approving prostitution, they support freedom of choice.

A12. The women's movement has argued for the rights of lesbians, and extends this position to include male homosexuals. (See 5.)

A13. The rights of women to control their own bodies will increase the pressure for birth control methods for women with fewer side effects and for the development of birth control methods for men.

A14. The right to abortion is part of women's rights to control their own bodies.

A17. More accessible abortion/contraception as well as personal freedom should make premarital intercourse more prevalent, but the numbers of sex partners may not increase. (See 7.)

B18. Masturbation among women should increase, more among older than adolescent women.

B19. Increased choice should lead to somewhat greater willingness to experiment sexually.

B20. Increases in premarital coitus, masturbation and other sexual practices should raise the total amount of sexual activity of women, but not necessarily that of men.

B21. An increase in sisterhood might increase homosexual experimentation among women but no changes are likely among men, even as a reaction to female equality.

C22. There may be some short-run increase in reaction to male-dominated sexuality, but this may be compensated for by a counter-movement into bisexuality among women. Little change will occur among males.

A23. As political-economic autonomy increases and women have equality, sexuality should be accompanied by greater pleasure.

B24. There is likely to be a modest increase in male sexual problems as women are more assertive and self-directing. As men become accustomed to a new state of affairs this should decline.

C26. Females should find more satisfaction, but males may suffer from change in social power.

B27. This should increase somewhat because women will be more assertive about their right to pleasure.

B28. As women are equal to men they may be more willing to change the conventional marriage contract with respect to sexual fidelity by both husbands and wives.

B29. Marriages held together only by economic circumstances would be more likely to dissolve; however, marriages contracted under conditions of equality may be more stable and rewarding.

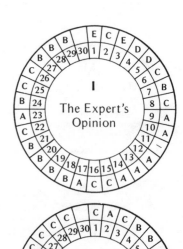

Development II*

A 2. The use of erotic material would be driven underground and private use would likely continue.

A 4. If nudity was thought to be obscene, then most sex acts themselves would be considered wrong as well.

B 5. Strong anti-obscenity laws would likely have some effects on general sex laws.

E 8. Many sex education materials would be directly affected by the law itself, and in general the social climate would be against sex education.

E10. Prostitution would continue to be illegal in a society that prohibited nudity.

D16. Certain kinds of sex research involving observation of sexual behavior or presentation of sexual stimuli would be prohibited.

D19. Prohibition of erotic materials could stigmatize sexual experimentation.

*The expert's opinions reflect the narrow impact of actions to control nudity; a national decision which would make nudity illegal, however, would probably be the result of a general conservative trend that would have far wider impacts.

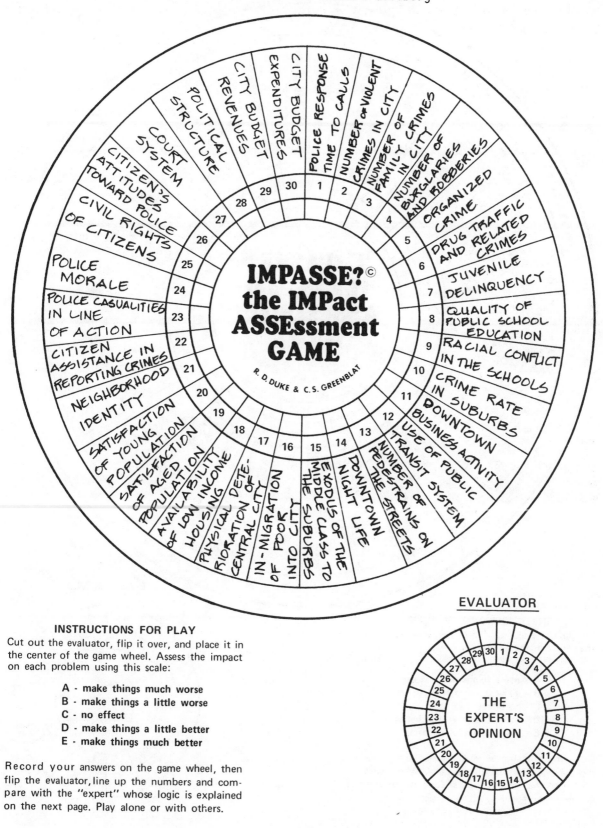

IMPASSE?© the IMPact ASSEssment GAME

R. D. DUKE & C.S. GREENBLAT

EVALUATOR

THE EXPERT'S OPINION

INSTRUCTIONS FOR PLAY

Cut out the evaluator, flip it over, and place it in the center of the game wheel. Assess the impact on each problem using this scale:

A - make things **much worse**
B - make things **a little worse**
C - **no effect**
D - make things **a little better**
E - make things **much better**

Record your answers on the game wheel, then flip the evaluator, line up the numbers and compare with the "expert" whose logic is explained on the next page. Play alone or with others.

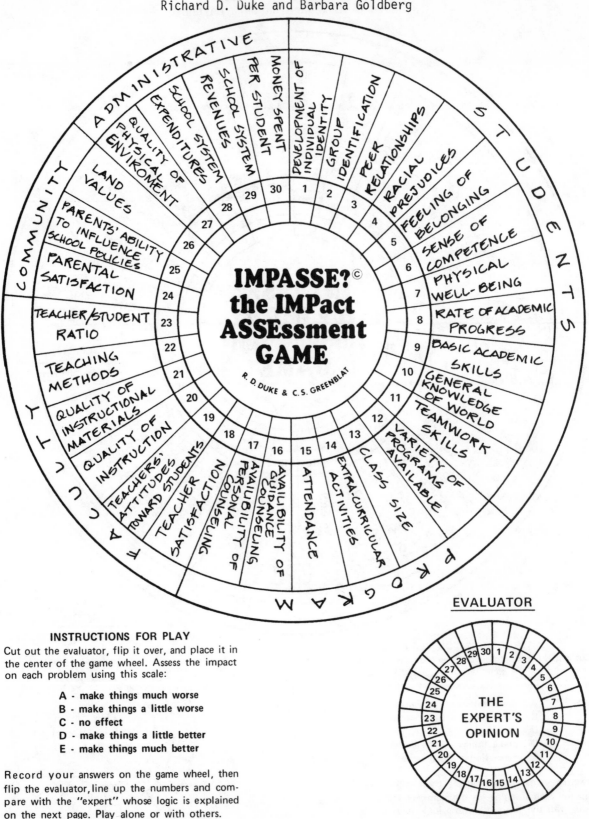

IMPASSE?© the IMPact ASSEssment GAME
R. D. DUKE & C. S. GREENBLAT

EVALUATOR

THE EXPERT'S OPINION

INSTRUCTIONS FOR PLAY

Cut out the evaluator, flip it over, and place it in the center of the game wheel. Assess the impact on each problem using this scale:

A - make things much worse
B - make things a little worse
C - no effect
D - make things a little better
E - make things much better

Record your answers on the game wheel, then flip the evaluator, line up the numbers and compare with the "expert" whose logic is explained on the next page. Play alone or with others.

AT-ISSUE! EXAMPLES

Overview.

Three examples of AT-ISSUE! are included here:

1. Regional Planning AT-ISSUE! by Richard D. Duke. This is a modification of a version of AT-ISSUE! prepared for use in Monterey Bay, California. Specific geographic references and details have been removed to make the game useful for many locales. Materials included are:

    A problem description for the operator to read aloud.

    A list of constituencies.

    A set of Issue Cards (one set is needed per team).

    A copy of the CROSS-IMPACTING wheel.

    A copy of the VALUE-ORDERING wheel.

    A copy of the VARIDENT wheel.

    A copy of the Perceived Impact form.

    A copy of the UPPER-LIMIT wheel.

There are instructions for running the game in section II. If you wish to play one Issue Card, it will be necessary to photocopy five copies of the Issue Cards, the CROSS-IMPACTING wheel, the VALUE-ORDERING wheel, the VARIDENT wheel, the Perceived Impact form and the UPPER-LIMIT wheel for each issue. If you wish to play through more than one Issue Card, it will be necessary to photocopy five additional copies of the CROSS-IMPACTING wheel, the VARIDENT wheel, the Perceived Impact form and the UPPER-LIMIT wheel for issue. Further copies of the VALUE-ORDERING wheel are not necessary, since values should remain constant throughout play.

2. Urban Problems AT-ISSUE! by Richard D. Duke and Cathy Greenblat.

   This is a modification of a 50 item IMPASSE? game developed by the two authors early in the design state of this trilogy. In its conversion to an AT-ISSUE! game, geographic references and details relevant to specific urban areas have been removed to make the material applicable to many locales.

   Use the same materials listed for Regional Planning AT-ISSUE!, excluding the UPPER-LIMIT wheel.

3. Family Dynamics AT-ISSUE! by Cathy S. Greenblat and Richard D. Duke.

   This is a new example created for this manual. A slight alteration of materials is demonstated in this version. Play options by members of an actual family and by simulated families are described. Materials included are:

   A game description and modified rules for play.

   An event list (for simulated families).

   A CROSS-IMPACTING wheel.

   A VARIDENT wheel.

   Photocopy 16 CROSS-IMPACTING wheels and 16 VARIDENT wheels. This will provide you with sufficient materials for a four person group (a real family or a group playing family members) to play four events. If more people are to play or more events are to be considered, more copies of the wheels will have to be made.

Description of the Problem.

Man generally has had only limited success in controlling the development
of urban regions. A variety of planning and management tools do exist and are
employed; these have grown more sophisticated over the past three decades. But
in spite of the methodology employed, or the vigorous efforts of the citizens
involved, or the best-intentioned efforts of those responsible for urban growth,
it is a rare region that does not exhibit serious flaws after development
occurs.

In those cases where development is rapid and where pressures for growth
are great, the negative impact of development is usually most severe. There
are at least four underlying causes for the ultimate dissatisfaction with the
product of rapid growth: (1) the speed of development often leaves too little
time for the necessary advance planning and coordination of effort, (2) the
interest of the developers is often a short-term, profit objective, and is too
narrowly focused on individual projects which compete with one another, (3) the
ultimate residents of the area are not present as viable partners in the
development process until after the construction is completed, (4) the enormous
complexity of an urban community often shields secondary and tertiary negative
effects until after the construction is completed.

A typical scenario, somewhat embellished, might present a highly desirable
and somewhat pristine area inhabited by local residents. For whatever reason,
the impetus for growth gets under way, perhaps triggered by new industry or the
growth of tourism or some similar phenomenon, and construction is undertaken
for a variety of new dwelling units. In successive waves these are occupied;
new jobs create the demand for new housing, which is also constructed and
occupied; as these waves of housing are built and occupied, ancillary land uses

are also constructed (schools, shopping centers, places of amusement, etc.).
When this process is rapid, it is entirely possible that the number of new
residents is greater than the number of original residents, giving way to a
curious phenomenon: the newly developed environment is to the liking of
neither the original residents who would prefer the previous tranquility, nor
the new residents who arrived after the development was completed. Values
incorporated into this morass are often predominately those of the developers
rather than those of the ultimate residents.

Effective urban planning must, of necessity, be oriented towards an
articulated goal-set as well as to a long-term perspective. As a consequence,
plans - while useful for establishing perspective - are somewhat limited in
guiding the individual decisions which are reached in the daily confrontation
between the developer and community. Because of the large number of issues
which arise in the process of development, there is inevitably a profusion of
coalitions which form to meet each threat, and then disband after the issue is
resolved. It is true that there is often a nucleus of citizens who are in the
center of each coalition. However, most citizen groups tend to be relatively
short-lived, and those which form because of a particular issue are likely to
include many new faces. The effectiveness of these coalitions is hindered by
their impermanence as well as by the large number of citizens engaged in the
dialogue. Because issues emerge, become heated and are resolved in relatively
short time-spans, some large segments of the population inevitably are not
engaged in the dialogue. Further, those who confront a particular issue are
generally only peripherally aware of related issues, prior decisions or pending
decisions which might be affected by or affect the issue at hand.

It is assumed that the planning staff for a developing region will employ
all of the known techniques, whether traditional or innovative, which are useful

for controlling rapid development. AT-ISSUE! is a game which represents a new technique for the planner's use, specifically oriented toward improving the quality of citizen dialogue on the issues of urban change.

In recent years, most people have become aware of the environmental degradation that results from man's haphazard utilization of resources. This increased consciousness has come along at the right moment. Technological change has never taken place so quickly and the ramifications of such change have never had such far-reaching effects. One area that feels this impact is the Monterey region of California. It is exceedingly beautiful, dangerously close to suffering major ecological disaster and has as great a growth potential as any region in the western United States. Clearly, the region could benefit by a systematic method of cataloging the far-reaching impacts of man's planned change in the environment. The 14 issues presented below are not the only issues in the region, nor are they necessarily the most important. They are, however, current and typical of the problems a region faces. They are used here to illustrate AT-ISSUE!

Proceed according to the instructions to the next step of play.

1. SUPERTANKER PORT

Should a port for supertankers be developed in the Bay? Yes____ No____

The Army Corps of Engineers is considering a harbor for "supertankers," displacing over 250,000 tons, which carry crude oil to underwater pipes leading to a refinery on shore. In their choice of a port, the Corps is looking for an area having relatively calm weather as well as necessary channel depth. Need for such tankers arises from the recent power shortage which forces the United States to rely on imported oil sources in large quantities.

A current study of the issue includes questions of need, environmental impact, legal feasibility, and possible alternatives. Danger from oil spills, legislation prohibiting oil drilling in the bay, effects on area ecosystems and refinery pollution must be balanced against the desirability of the location and the need for larger tankers.

2. REGIONAL SHOPPING CENTER

Should a major regional shopping center be constructed? Yes____ No____

The shopping center would include a 120-acre auto dealership and two major department stores (with eventual expansion to include a third) which will form the initial nucleus. The two-level complex will house both subsidiary shops and the department stores inside a single, enclosed, air-conditioned mall.

Contractors expect the center to absorb an additional 450,000 square feet by 1979 with another 200,000 square feet by 1982.

Construction of the center is expected further the movement toward a tourist-oriented fringe shopping areas. This, as well as the competition with existing shopping centers are factors to be considered in the decision.

3. COASTAL SUPERHIGHWAY CONSTRUCTION

Should a superhighway be constructed along the coast? Yes____ No____

When finished, the freeway will link with the interstate system. Included in this project is construction of the major connecting streets.

Easier flow of traffic may induce development in areas which oppose growth, as well as in area which desire expansion. The need for and the convenience of the highway should be examined in light of increased traffic congestion, aesthetic considerations, impact on growth and the feasibility of alternatives such as a public transit system.

4. SWAMP WILDLIFE SANCTUARY

Should coastal swampland areas be reserved for wildlife sanctuaries and protected from intrusion by developments? Yes____ No____

Contractors have plans for developing a swamp site long known as a sanctuary for rare transient birds and a home for many other species of local wildlife. Development is planned so that 175 units of 2-story townhouses will be concentrated in the northeastern portion of the area, leaving the remaining land – including the swamp – as open space. In spite of assurances by the development company that the project will include a scenic easement in order to protect the marsh, citizens have voiced reservations concerning the project and want the Park Disrict to purchase the land as open space. The price of $15,000 per acre is much too high for the district to pay.

5. RESTRICTED COASTLINE BUILDING

Should legislation restricting coastline building be repealed? Yes____ No____

Legislation currently restricting development within 1000 yards of the ocean front has the intent of maintaining the natural beauty and ecological balance of the area's coastal habitats. As a result, contractors often decide to build elsewhere, or they attempt to circumvent the legislation by applying for exemptions.

Urban planners are concerned that overemphasis on the environment may (1) hurt tourism and (2) produce an area in which only the extremely wealthy can live. Conservationists, on the other hand, claim that overdevelopment will destroy any attraction the area has for tourists as well as residents.

6. GROWTH OF TOURISM

Should rapid growth of the tourist industry be encouraged (for example: public expenditure to save a scenic "Old Town" area)? Yes____ No____

Last year, over $106 million was brought into the region by convention delegates, and the total tourist industry (visitors as well as conventions) created 4,440,000 man-hours of work. Because of the area's economic dependence on tourism, much pressure exists for developing tourist attractions and for construction of restaurants, conference centers and coastline hotels. Current city plans are designed to make down-town more tourist-oriented, and to move local business to the fringes of the city limits. Residents are concerned that tourism is being emphasized at the expense of local residents, scenery, environment and historical heritage.

7. COMBINED REGIONAL SEWERAGE SYSTEM

Should a regional sewerage system be implemented rather than multiple local sewerage treatment projects? Yes____ No____

The Association of Area Governments has proposed a giant inland sewerage treatment and disposal system which will eventually include the entire County. Construction costs of $45 million cover the plant and major interceptors used to provide tertiary treatment including nutrient removal and filtration. Liquids would be discharged onto the fields during summer and fall and into the river during the rest of the year. Because of delays in implementation and feelings by some localities that their facilities are adequate, the regional plan has met with opposition in spite of substantial federal and state backing (up to 87.5%).

8. AIRPORT EXPANSION

Should airport capacity be expanded through programmed development of facilities? Yes____ No____

Concerns involve growth of the airport itself and zoning of surrounding areas. The former includes need for and cost of new facilities, increased population and traffic flow, easing of overcrowded facilities in passenger and freight areas, and eventual effects on noise and smog levels.
The latter is a question of land use. For safety's sake, the State Director of Aeronautics has suggested a "buffer zone" surrounding airport grounds. Presently, 1200 homes and a major shopping center are planned for this area. Expansion of the airport will increase the conflict between developers and zoning restrictions.

9. NEW CONFERENCE COMPLEX

Should construction of a large hotel/conference center be permitted? Yes____ No____

The City Urban Renewal Agency is planning to build a 300-room Sheraton hotel along with a conference center containing a 1400 seat theater, ballroom and exhibition facilities. Its location in the middle of an area of historically valuable houses creates a great deal of controversy even though the complex will attract convention business. The fact that it is designed by non-local architects, questions about the extent of resident interest in the arts and environmental costs are all part of the issue.

10. HIGH DENSITY DEVELOPMENT OF FARM LAND

Should major land areas be rezoned for intensive, planned housing developments? Yes____ No____

One major farm extends 292 acres both east and west of the highway. As surrounding areas were developed, complaints arose indicating that chemicals used as fertilizer for crops were affecting water supplies in nearby housing complexes. The owners of the farm have agreed to sell their property.

Among alternative uses for the land are land-disposal, partial or full retention as open space, low-density development and high-density development. A plan approved by the County Board of Supervisors calls for a 300-unit hotel and 298 residential units on the eastern acreage, while the western part would be retained as open space, but the City Council is fighting this plan. The fight centers around an environmental impact report which the Council feels does not adequately discuss consequences of population increase.

11. PRE-EMPTIVE REGIONAL PLANNING AGENCY

Should planning for growth be under the control of regional rather than local agencies? Yes____ No____

The region is a conglomeration of cities and towns sharing resources, services and industries; yet each of them deals with a unique population with specific needs. Since the cities together compose the "peninsula region," one would expect them to cooperate in legislative action without interfering with each city's individuality. This has become more of an ideal than a reality because the legislation in this region is difficult to pass and even more difficult to propose.

Voters have turned toward regional forms of government out of desperation. Passage of legislation restricting coastline building and creating Park and Open Space District indicate that the residents feel that local government has not protected them against creeping forms of commercialism. At the same time, there are many who feel that the citizens within each community are better able to deal with their problems than a remotely placed state or federal government.

12. SUBSIDIZED MIGRANT WORKER CENTER

Should a publicly subsidized center be developed to care for the needs of migrant workers? Yes____ No____

Migrant workers make up a substantial segment of the area's population and they compose the backbone of the agriculture industry, one of the region's largest revenue producer. They have their own unique demands as a minority group, but they are widely scattered throughout the peninsula and are not well-organized. As a result, little legislation directly influencing the migrant workers is passed.

Because of past fraud and incompetance, much money has been spent on migrant workers' problems with little result. Any new programs face several challenges. They must: regain lost confidence, avoid interfering with existing training programs, deal with federal bureaucracy and lack of funds.

13. OPEN SPACE ACQUISITION PROGRAM

Should a public agency be empowered to coordinate and control the acquisition of open space in the region? Yes____ No____

One of the functions of such an agency would be to accept gifts of real and personal property for public use. Another function would be the use of tax monies to acquire endangered areas such as the swamp wildlife sanctuary. Monies might also be used for acquisition of lakes and land which must be sold. It is unclear whether the current budget allotted to such an agency allows it to operate in more than a token fashion; most of the land is priced above the agency's budget.

14. LOCATION OF LOW-INCOME HOUSING

Should scattered-site, low-income housing developments of limited size be distributed through residential neighborhoods? Yes____ No____

While recognizing a growing need for moderate and low income housing, planners are finding difficulty in locating areas with the requisite zoning. Most of the available open areas are in the Central Valley region, but the population protest the destruction of the natural setting in which they live. Present zoning, while preserving open areas and emphasizing single unit dwellings, prohibits an influx of younger families with school-age children, and discriminates against elderly people on fixed incomes and other low-income groups.

15. (short title) _____

Question: _____

_____ Yes____ No____

Description: _____

_____

_____

_____

_____

_____

_____

REGIONAL PLANNING

Group Name _____

The wheel diagram "AT-ISSUE! CROSS-IMPACTING" by R. D. Duke & C. S. Greenblat contains the following issues arranged in segments (numbered 1–15), each with A, B, C rings:

1. **SUPERTANKER PORT** — Should a port for supertankers be developed in Monterey Bay?
2. **SHOPPING CENTER** — Should a major regional shopping center be constructed?
3. **COASTAL SUPERHIGHWAY** — Should a superhighway be constructed along the coast?
4. **WILDLIFE SANCTUARY** — Should coastal swampland areas be reserved for wildlife sanctuaries and protected from intrusion by developments?
5. **COASTLINE BUILDING** — Should legislation restricting coastline building be repealed?
6. **GROWTH OF TOURISM** — Should rapid growth of the tourist industry be encouraged? (for example: public expenditures to save Cannery Row)
7. **SEWERAGE SYSTEM** — Should a regional sewerage system be implemented rather than multiple local sewerage treatment projects?
8. **AIRPORT EXPANSION** — Should airport capacity be expanded through programmed development of facilities?
9. **CONFERENCE COMPLEX** — Should construction of a large hotel/conference center be permitted?
10. **RANCH DEVELOPMENT** — Should major ranches be re-zoned for intensive, planned housing developments?
11. **GROWTH PLANNING** — Should planning for growth be under the control of regional rather than local agencies?
12. **MIGRANT WORKER** — Should a publicly subsidized center be developed to care for the needs of migrant workers?
13. **LOW-INCOME HOUSING** — Should scattered-site low-income housing developments of limited size be distributed through residential neighborhoods?
14. **OPEN SPACE AQUISITION** — Should a public agency be empowered to coordinate and control the acquisition of open space in the Monterey region?
15. **ADD YOUR OWN ISSUE**

INSTRUCTIONS FOR PLAY

Assess the impact of this issue resolution on all other issues:

A = increased probability of the issue being resolved AFFIRMATIVELY

B = increased probability of the issue being resolved NEGATIVELY

C = NO IMPACT

Issue No. _____   Issue Name _____

_____ Affirmative Resolution   _____ Negative Resolution

REGIONAL PLANNING

Group Name _____

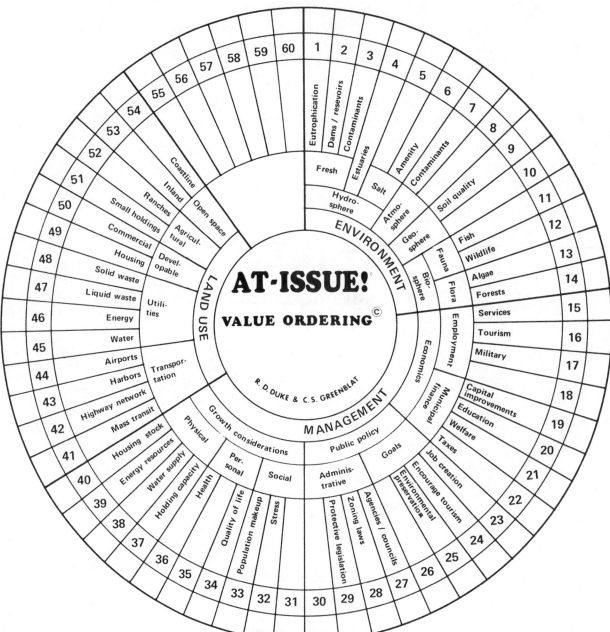

INSTRUCTIONS FOR PLAY

Assign 100 points among the variables, in multiples of 10. These points should indicate the things you most care about. If you would like to see the item increase (e.g., per cent of budget used for schools) put a plus (+) sign in front of your weight. If you would like to see the item decrease (e.g., property tax) put a minus (−) sign in front of the weight

These weights will apply throughout the game so assign them with some care.

REGIONAL PLANNING

Group Name _____

AT-ISSUE!

VARIDENT ©

the VARIable
IDENTification
game

R. D. DUKE & C. S. GREENBLAT

ENVIRONMENT

Eutrophication
Dams / resevoirs
Contaminants
Fresh
Estuaries
Salt
Hydro-sphere
Amenity
Atmo-sphere
Contaminants
Geo-sphere
Soil quality
Fish
Fauna
Wildlife
Bio-sphere
Flora
Algae
Forests
Services
Employment
Tourism
Military
Economics
Capital improvements
Municipal
finance
Education
Welfare
Taxes
Goals
Job creation
Encourage tourism
Environmental preservation
Agencies / councils
Zoning laws
Protective legislation
Administrative
Public policy

MANAGEMENT

Growth considerations
Physical
Personal
Social
Quality of life
Population makeup
Stress
Health
Holding capacity
Water supply
Energy resources
Housing stock
Mass transit
Highway network
Harbors
Airports
Water
Energy
Utilities
Liquid waste
Solid waste
Housing
Commercial
Developable
Small holdings
Agricultural
Ranches
Inland
Open space
Coastline

LAND USE

INSTRUCTIONS FOR PLAY

Assess the impact on each variable using this scale:

  +2   make things much better
  +1   make things a little better
    0   no effect
  −1   make things a little worse
  −2   make things much worse

On the reverse side add any comments you consider appropriate.

REGIONAL PLANNING

Group Name _____

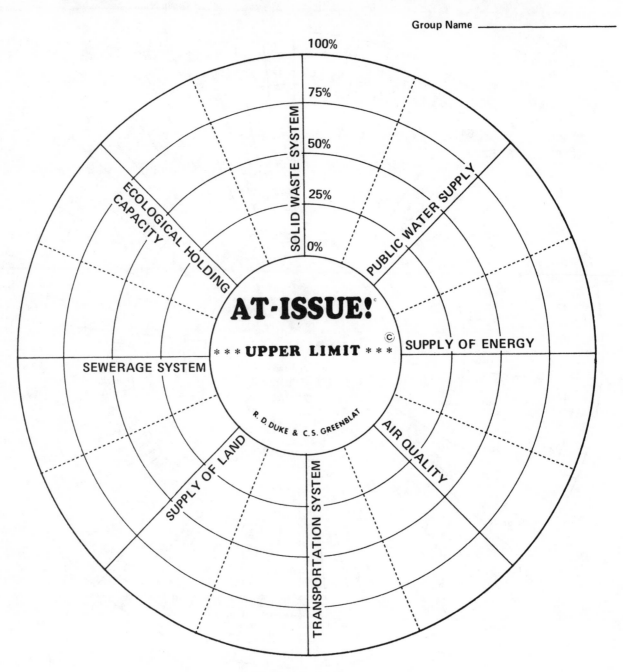

Labels on the wheel (clockwise from top): SOLID WASTE SYSTEM, PUBLIC WATER SUPPLY, SUPPLY OF ENERGY, AIR QUALITY, TRANSPORTATION SYSTEM, SUPPLY OF LAND, SEWERAGE SYSTEM, ECOLOGICAL HOLDING CAPACITY.

Scale markings: 0%, 25%, 50%, 75%, 100%

Center: AT-ISSUE! *** UPPER LIMIT *** R. D. DUKE & C. S. GREENBLAT

INSTRUCTIONS FOR PLAY

1. Mark each variable to indicate the current level of use (to what extent is the system already burdened?). Connect all marks to form a circle.
2. Repeat with a different colored pencil, BUT mark each variable as you expect it to be five years from now, based on the stated resolution of the issue under discussion.

Urban Problems AT-ISSUE!   Richard D. Duke and Cathy S. Greenblat

Description of the Problem.

What images come to mind when you hear the term "city?" Most of us conjure up conflicting sets of pictures. On one hand, we think of "the city" as a place of excitement, diversity and opportunity; we immediately understand the refrain "How're ya gonna keep them down on the farm, after they've seen Paris?" On the other hand, we think of the brutality, danger, squalor and the anonymity present in many cities and of the inability of the average resident to cope with these conditions, and we wonder how much exaggeration there is in portrayals such as Jules Pfeiffer's movie *Little Murders.*

Both sets of images have some truth, and they stem from the same underlying sources. High population and high density, for example, contribute to overcrowding and anonymity, but also to a heterogenous population, availability of cultural enterprises that would not be economically feasible in less populous areas, and the ability to "do your own thing" with little interference from others. Therefore, an array of benefits can be lined up next to an array of problems. At present, the "problem orientation" seems to dominate. Prophets of doom abound, sounding alarms about the plight of the cities, and offering shibboleths about deterioration, "sick" cities, "dying" cities, etc.

But what actually is meant by an "urban problem?" The term seems simple and obvious at first glance, but further questioning reveals lack of clarity. A social problem exists because there is a significant discrepancy between the standards people have and the reality of the situation, not because of the violation of some *inherent* standard. If, for example, everyone expected a ten minute wait for the dial tone when they use the phone or a three hour ride to cross the city, present communication and transportation conditions would be considered extremely good. Energies and resources would be directed to other urban concerns and "problems."

The general lack of agreement on the definition of the most pressing urban problems is not surprising. People located in different places in the social structure are likely to develop different standards and to perceive the same situation differently. Consequently, ideas about whether something is a problem, how serious it is, and how important it is relative to other problems vary from person to person, group to group, and area to area. For some, ethnic and racial residential segregation is a "problem" because it means differential access to the educational resources of the city. For others, segregation gives the reassurance that they can be with their "own kind" and take advantage of supportive mechanisms within the community; a *breakdown* of residential barriers would be defined as the problem. The flow of consumers to suburban shopping centers which provide easier parking and less traffic congestion is a serious "problem" to downtown merchants and the city Chamber of Commerce, but is a delight to suburban proprietors and to harried shoppers.

Surely there are some commonly identified problems present in varying degrees from one city to the next. How can we identify these? One answer is to ask what a city is, and to find the "problems" in the list of characteristics thus generated. Social commentators and social scientists seeking the defining attributes of cities suggest the following characteristics among others: (a) a high population of people with heterogenous backgrounds and characteristics; (b) high population density; (c) a complex division of labor, largely excluding agricultural endeavors; (d) a role as transportation and communication hub for a larger region; (e) a focal point for religious, political and cultural enterprises; (f) a distinctive "way of life" for residents, marked by anonymity, fragmented personal relations and impersonality. These and other possible descriptors unfortunately help us little in defining as positive or negative, depending upon the evaluator's values and preferences. For the lonely person seeking intimate relations with others, the "anonymity" of city life is a problem; for one seeking to pursue a deviant life style, that anonymity is a benefit deriving from city life.

A more fruitful approach to the definition and delineation of urban problems and their interconnection is to focus upon the functions of a city. Then we can ask what is working well and what is not. The city is a system - an organism. Like any other social group or social system, it must, to continue, perform six basic tasks. These separate, though interconnected, requirements constitute the major areas of organized social activity for societal continuity, and represent formal frameworks or structures within which the daily lives of system members are enacted.

First, the population has to be reproduced, either through recruitment or reproduction. Unless new members are gained as old ones move out or die, the unit will be unable to continue. Imbalances or major shifts in the proportions of young and old, male and female may also create problems.

Second, the new members must be socialized into functioning members of society. Children must be provided with the values, skills, techniques and understanding which allow them to operate successfully in the system; adult members who have immigrated from other places must likewise be taught the value and norm framework and how to function within it.

Third, steps must be taken to insure the mental and physical health of the population.

Fourth, order must be maintained, through formal and informal regulations. In addition to maintaining order within the group - in this case the city - steps must be taken to insure order between the group and external systems - other cities, the region, the state and the nation.

Fifth, goods and services must be produced and distributed. There must be some sort of division of labor, a set of norms regarding private and public ownership, a system of allocating scarce resources.

Sixth, members must be given meaning and motivation. Without some sense of meaning and purpose of life within the system, they will not be motivated to continue to live as members and to meet their responsibilities. "Satisfactory" conditions of life, sufficient respite from problems and work, and patterned sets of explanations of "what it's all about" must be provided.

Our most critical urban problems can be viewed in terms of failures to successfully meet these six functions of population reproduction, socialization, health maintenance, production and distribution of goods and services, maintenance of internal and external order and provision of meaning and motivation. The functional problems selected for this AT-ISSUE! game represent those problems on which we think there is fairly widespread agreement that they constitute "problems." They are more than irritations; they are indicative of system malfunctions. Despite the vigorous actions being taken to deal with some of them, they seem to be intensifying.

An understanding of the complex elements that create, sustain and feed such problems, and of the difficulties of their solution emerges more clearly if the problems are viewed as interrelated. It is not just that increases in one lead to increases in some others, or that "solutions" vie for scarce funds, but that *a "solution" to one problem may intensify another problem.* Since most policies and programs have secondary and tertiary, as well as direct effects, atomistic consideration allows little headway in understanding urban dilemmas; the implications of proposed solutions must be viewed broadly. By assessing the impact of a proposed solution to a problem on the *entire* gamut of problems, perhaps we can assure that we do not come to an impasse in our cities.

1. AIR POLLUTION

Should the Public Power Plant be allowed to burn coal or high-sulphur oil? Yes___ No___

In the recent energy crisis, Public Power asked for and received permission to temporarily burn coal in place of low-sulphur oil mandated by governmental restrictions. Though the crisis was over before coal-burning was underway, future developments (oil shortage, price of oil, availability of low-sulphur oil, the economic problems faced by the utility company) may require the same decision.

Consider: By-products in the air from fossil-fuel power generation; alternative sources of electrical energy; capital and operating expenses; governmental subsidy.

2. REPEAL RENT CONTROL LAW

Should the rent control law be repealed? Yes___ No___

Under the proposed "vacancy decontrol" bill, vacated apartments would no longer be subject to rent controls, and landlords would be able to set any rent that the market would bear. The Governor has proposed that rents be rolled back to January 1977 and that in the future landlords and tenants negotiate rents which could be appealed to a city rent board. Tenant groups believe this approach does not give them enough protection; landlords claim it imposes economic hardships.

Consider: Impact of housing shortage; effect of rent upon population movement; controls vs. free market; inflationary spiral.

3. INDUSTRIAL DEVELOPMENT

Should incentives be created to encourage more industrial development? Yes___ No___

The city has large undeveloped and decayed areas many of which border navigable waterways. Local industry provides convenient jobs for the growing population. Different industries generate different amounts and types of jobs, truck traffic, pollutants and visual impact on adjacent communities. Through zoning, land write-down, provision of municipal services or facilities, industries can be attracted.

Consider: The need for industrial jobs; the improved tax base; type of labor-pool attracted; pollutants; alternative uses of and priorities for the water-front land.

4. SANITARY LANDFILL

Should the sanitary landfill be closed? Yes____ No____

The sanitary landfill has already been filled beyond original plans but can be used for 10-15 more years. Filling continues because alternative means of solid waste disposal are more expensive, only experimental in nature, or objected to by more effective political entities. Residents, for example, successfully stopped fill operations in "Bay Park" marsh. A long period of settlement is required before the landfill can be developed for other uses because of the instability of the land and escaping methane gas.

Consider: Alternative solutions to solid waste disposal; source of funds for research/development or to pay higher disposal costs; ecological/bacteriological factors; need for moratorium so that development can take place sooner.

5. GREENBELT PRESERVATION

Should a "special zoning district" control the future of the city's greenbelt as a natural area? Yes____ No____

Though much of the greenbelt is now publicly owned, its future may be in jeopardy as green space. Part of Frederick Law Olmsted's century-old plan, the greenbelt has been proposed as the route for the "Olmsted Trailway," a multi-faceted recreational network. The land is highly desirable for homes and the value has increased since High Rock Girl Scout Camp, adjacent to the greenbelt, was sold to, and then saved from tract developers.

Consider: Need for natural green space; need for more housing; tract development's impact on natural features; economic implications for current and future land owners; the effects of planned development: cluster housing, research parks, cemeteries, transfer of development rights, etc.

6. GREENBELT PARKWAY

Should the greenbelt be the primary route of the new expressway?
Yes____ No____

An old controversy is once again in the headlines: it is proposed that the parkway be built along the original route through the greenbelt but with parallel bicycle paths to satisfy objections of environmentalists. The largely developed natural greenbelt is comprised of both publicly and privately owned land, much of the latter under control of the Boy Scouts and the Country Club.

Consider: The gasoline shortage; open-space needs; alternate highway routes and/or forms of transportation; destruction of residential communities; widening of local arteries; compatibility of bicyclists, hikers, and automobiles; air and noise pollution.

7. NORTH SHORE TRANSIT

Should the present "North Shore" railroad right-of-way be reactivated for use by passenger traffic? Yes____ No____

Until a few years ago, the city's mass transit facilities included a "North Shore" line which is now used only for freight. It has been proposed that the existing right-of-way and some of the neglected station structures, etc. be reactivated and improved to provide easy access to the Ferry terminal as well as to industrial sites at the west end of the rail link. The line has much greater capacity than current projections of riders and not enough people are within walking distance to insure profitable or even breakeven operation.

Consider: Need for public transportation; convenience of stations to riders and destinations; possibility of free bus-train transfers; possibility of free bus-train transfers to increase ridership; speed and cost of start-up; bus-lanes.

8. CENTRAL CITY PARK REHABILITATION

Should $10 million be spent over the next ten years for the rehabilitation of Central City Park? Yes____ No____

Central City Park is considered by some to be the prize urban park in the nation. Over the years overuse, misuse and lack of proper and sufficient maintenance has caused it to fall into a state of enormous disrepair. A major survey and rehabilitation program over the next ten years has been proposed. Proponents argue that the park serves regional as well as local needs. Opponents believe the money should be spent on other city parks or other capital improvement projects.

Consider: Irreplaceability of natural specimens; damage to ecosystem; park and recreational needs vs. other capital needs; Central City Park vs. other parks.

9. "OLDTOWN" RESTORATION

Should the growth of a tourist industry around the "Oldtown" Restoration be encouraged? Yes____ No____

"Oldtown" Restoration is a collection of original historic buildings and artifacts which have been gathered together at a picturesque site in the center of the city. It has been proposed that the hotel facilities be developed as part of the oldtown restoration in order to encourage longer visits by tourists from all parts of the country. The idea presupposes adequate parking, shopping and restaurants to serve the needs of the increased number of visitors, most of whom can be expected to come by automobile.

Consider: Oldtown's ability to attract a national audience; the impact of more visitors, more business income, more jobs; effect of hotels, etc. on adjacent communities.

10. HIGH RISE DEVELOPMENT

Should the area around the Central City Mall be developed as a satellite city center? Yes____ No____

The Mall is designed for future commercial and office building expansion. 2400 condominium high-rise apartments are proposed on the adjacent 65 acres. The city has approved higher density zoning in exchange for developer's concessions: sewage treatment plant, 17 acres of open space, 4 acres for an elementary school. Adjacent residents oppose the project: high density, lack of municipal services, aesthetics.

Consider: Alternate uses for the project's site; educational/shopping/recreational needs of both project's and area's residents; appropriateness of high-rise construction; impact of developer's concessions on City's development costs.

11. LOW-INCOME HOUSING

Should scatter-site low-income housing be built when government subsidies again become available? Yes____ No____

The working poor, the elderly and those on a fixed income need low-rent housing. The private sector has stated over and over again that high construction costs make low-rent housing impossible without heavy governmental subsidy. Midtown has the largest amount of land available for development in the city. Some believe that small low-rent projects scattered in stable existing communities provide a healthier social mix between old-time and newer residents. Others fear a large influx of strangers, decreasing property values and crime.

Consider: The housing needs of low-income population; the condition of existing housing; social and economic integration; neighborhood values; appearance of low-rent projects; other means of housing available, for example, skewed rents.

12. SPECIAL ZONING

Should a special zoning district be created to control the future of the "Little Europe" community? Yes____ No____

The "Little Europe" community is a neighborhood of many ethnic groups, low income housing and local shops. Pressures for additional high rise office and apartment development threaten the existing social fabric. The city has proposed a special zoning district to preserve the community's flavor, but it would limit the rights of landowners and developers by imposing additional height limitations.

Consider: Desirability of preserving unique communities; economic implications for present and future land owners and developers; freedom vs. governmental controls.

13. ELEMENTARY SCHOOL GRADES

Should West Side elementary schools include grades normally assigned to junior high schools? Yes____ No____

Junior-high schools are notorious for overcrowding, concentration of students lacking in basic skills, use of drugs and for acute behavior problems. Many middle-class families, largely white, whose children attend neighborhood public elementary schools, send their junior-high school age children to private schools. Consequently, the junior-high schools have a higher percentage on non-white children. Their parents have proposed that the neighborhood elementary schools use available space to retain their 7th grade classes rather than graduating children into the junior-high schools.

Consider: Neighborhood schools; racial and economic integration; improvements in public education; permanency of proposed solutions; economical school space utilization.

14. LIMITING DEVELOPMENT

Should limits be placed on the pace of the city's "Cross-River" area development? Yes____ No____

The city's "Cross-River" area has grown rapidly since the opening of the "Cross-River" Bridge: 26,324 new families in nine years! Large areas remain undeveloped and available for several thousand *more* families. A cynical proposal for control is to impose high tolls on inbound moving vans; another, more serious idea is to refuse to permit new housing unless adequate services are provided.

Consider: Need for new housing; the problems of density; the quality of life; economic considerations: land speculation, taxes and jobs; rights of current residents vs. the needs of newcomers; freedom vs. government controls.

15. (short title)_____

Question_____

_____Yes____ No____

Description_____

_____

_____

_____

_____

_____

URBAN PROBLEMS   Group Name _____

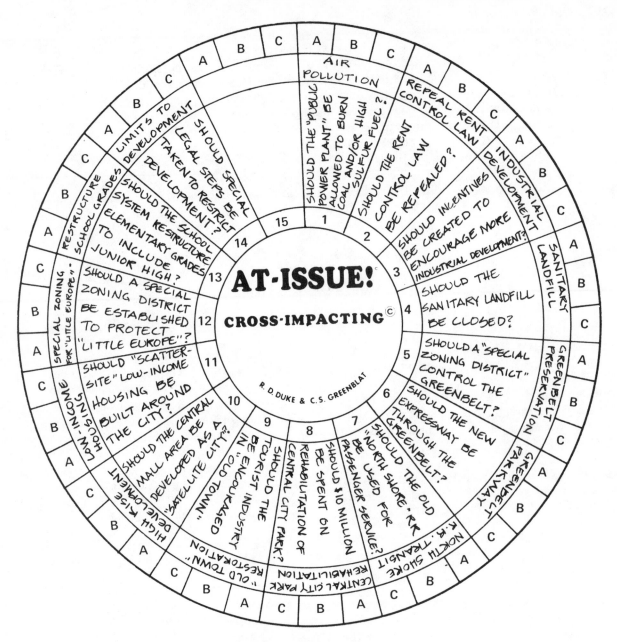

INSTRUCTIONS FOR PLAY

Assess the impact of this issue resolution on all other issues:

A = increased probability of the issue being resolved AFFIRMATIVELY

B = increased probability of the issue being resolved NEGATIVELY

C = NO IMPACT

Issue No. _____   Issue Name _____

_____ Affirmative Resolution   _____ Negative Resolution

AT-ISSUE!

VALUE ORDERING ©

R. D. DUKE & C. S. GREENBLAT

Sector labels: GOVERNMENT, DEMOGRAPHIC, RESIDENTIAL POPULATIONS, EMPLOYMENT, CRIME/JUSTICE, SOCIAL/PSYCHOLOGICAL, ENVIRONMENTAL, TRANSPORTATION, HEALTH, SERVICES, EDUCATION, OTHER

Selected numbered variables (outer ring):

1 Proportion Aged
2 Exodus of Middle Class to Suburbs
3 Immigration, Poor, Uneducated, Unskilled
4 Mobility Rate of Population
5 Scarcity, Cost of Housing
6 Racial Restrictions on Housing
7 Rate of Housing Demolition
8 Urban Sprawl
9 Condition of Inner City Housing
10 Discriminatory Practices
11 Minority Rate of Unemployment
12 Number of Unskilled Jobs Available
13 Cost of Living
14 Tax
15 Economic Health of Central Business District
16 Crime Rate in Inner City
17 Drug Traffic
18 Organized Crime
18 White Collar Crime
19 Political Graft & Corruption
20 Efficiency of Court System
21 Pace of Life
22 Rate of Mental Illness
23 Rate of Suicide
24 Willingness to Get Personality Involved
25 Religious Activity
26 Sense of Community
27 Air, Water, Noise Pollution
28 Solid Waste Disposal
29 Visual Environment
30 Graffiti, Vandalism
31 Costs
32 Commuter Tax Revenues
33 Traffic Congestion
34 Availability of Parking Facilities
35 Roads
36 Quality of Medical Costs
37 Availability of Family Planning Facilities
38 Care of Handicapped
39 Availability & Quality of Hospital Care
40 Drug Rehabilitation
41 Care for Aged Dependent
42 Day Care Facilities
43 Pre-School Education
44 Educational Opportunities
45 Racial Conflict in Schools
46 Vocational Training
47 Classroom Capacity in Colleges
48 Quality of School Facilities
49 Private School Revenues
50 Fire Protection
51 Cultural Facilities
52 Recreational Facilities
53 Welfare Costs
54 General Costs
55 City Revenue Sources
56 Tax Base of City
57 Regional Government
58 Fragmented Political Power
59 Ingrained Bureaucracy
60 Structure Nues (Revenue-Expend)

INSTRUCTIONS FOR PLAY

Assign 100 points among the variables, in multiples of 10. These points should indicate the things you most care about. If you would like to see the item increase (e.g., per cent of budget used for schools) put a plus (+) sign in front of your weight. If you would like to see the item decrease (e.g., property tax) put a minus (−) sign in front of the weight

These weights will apply throughout the game so assign them with some care.

-81-

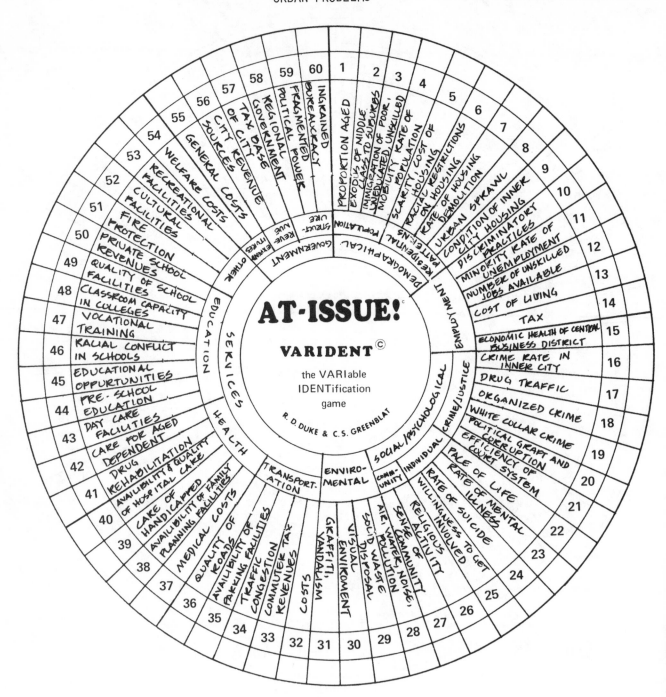

INSTRUCTIONS FOR PLAY

Assess the impact on each variable using this scale:

+2 make things much better
+1 make things a little better
0 no effect
−1 make things a little worse
−2 make things much worse

On the reverse side add any comments you consider appropriate.

-82-

Family Dynamics AT-ISSUE!   Cathy S. Greenblat and Richard D. Duke

This version of AT-ISSUE! is a simple one designed for play by real family members in a group or by non-related people simulating members of a family. In either instance, the purpose is to offer a means for intensive, systematic consideration of the impact of possible events on a number of elements of family life, as these impacts are perceived by the different members. For those simulating family life, AT-ISSUE! provides a way of exploring the idea of different views of the same event as it impacts on a family group. In the case of a real family, such a procedure also aims at opening and improving communications.

How to play Family Dynamics AT-ISSUE!

If you are members of a real family, you will probably wish to play yourselves. Alternatively, after playing a few events you may wish to switch and play one another, attempting to look at the problem through the eyes of someone else and rating each other later on how well you understood that perspective.

In the case of simulated families, players should divide into groups of four players, each group representing a family. Each player should assume one of the roles (mother, father, two children), and assign himself (or do so by group decision) the characteristics on the role cards. When these characteristics are decided, they should be communicated to others in the "family" group. Play proceeds as follows:

1. *Issue Definition* - Fifteen blank index cards should be distributed
    approximately evenly among the players. Each person should write on
    his or her index cards a short title and description of an event that
    might happen, that he or she would *like to see* happen or that he or
    she would *like to avoid* happening. Some examples are offered below.

-83-

They can be used as they are or can be modified; they should be supplimented with cards representing the player's ideas.

2. *Loading the CROSS-IMPACTING Wheel* - When all 15 cards have been filled out, they should be put together in a pack, and as one person reads them aloud, the players should each copy the titles into a copy of the CROSS-IMPACTING wheel. If photocopying facilities are available, it will be possible to "load" one copy and photocopy the rest.

3. *Issue Selection* - Select one issue (card) to play first. Do this by vote or by random choice. Since a normal "run" of Family Dynamics AT-ISSUE! will entail at least four cards being played, each person should have a chance to choose an issue, if turns are taken.

4. *CROSS-IMPACTING* - Each person should take a copy of the CROSS-IMPACTING wheel and follow the instructions on it.

5. *Discussion* - When all players have done the cross-impacting, there should be a short discussion of the responses each gave and the logic behind their responses.

6. *VARIDENT* - Each person should now consider the issue in terms of the variables in the VARIDENT wheel, following the instructions on the form.

7. *Discussion* - The last and most important step is to discuss similarities and differences in the assessments each player gave to the impact of the event. Can the group achieve a sense of whether this event would be generally positive or negative for the family as a whole?

Now go back to step three. Using a clean copy of the CROSS-IMPACTING wheel (loaded) and a clean copy of the VARIDENT wheel, consider another event.

Examples of events for Family Dynamics AT-ISSUE!

1. Previously non-working wife takes a full-time job.

2. Working wife receives a promotion to a job at a salary equal to that of her husband.

3. A serious temporary illness of one family member causes $5000 budget deficit in family finances.

4. New baby!

5. Husband agrees to take on 1/2 responsibility for domestic and childrearing tasks.

6. Child #1 or #2 "graduates" out of the family environment and goes on his or her own.

7. Husband offered a promotion which entails bringing about three hours of work home every evening.

8. Wife's lottery ticket pays her $20,000 cash.

9. Child #1 or #2's boyfriend (or girlfriend) requests to move into the family home.

10. Aged parent (grandparent) requests to move in.

Role Cards for use with simulated families.

FATHER

Employment status:

    employed____   unemployed____
        type of job_____
        full-time____
        part-time____
        weekly take-home pay_____

Other important data:

MOTHER

Employment status:

    employed____   unemployed____
        type of job_____
        full-time____
        part-time____
        weekly take-home pay____

Other important data:

CHILD #1

Sex____   Age____   School grade_____

Other important data:

CHILD #2

Sex____   Age____   School grade_____

Other important data:

Group Name _____

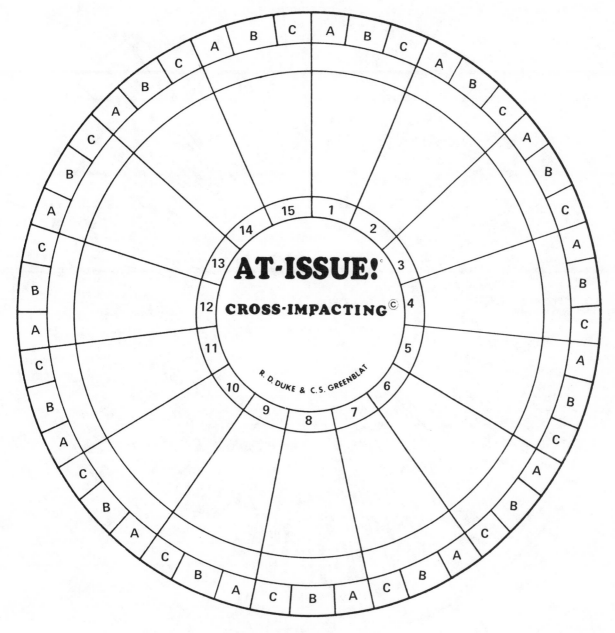

INSTRUCTIONS FOR PLAY

Assess the impact of this issue resolution on all other issues:

A = increased probability of the issue being resolved AFFIRMATIVELY

B = increased probability of the issue being resolved NEGATIVELY

C = NO IMPACT

Issue No. _____   Issue Name _____

_____ Affirmative Resolution   _____ Negative Resolution

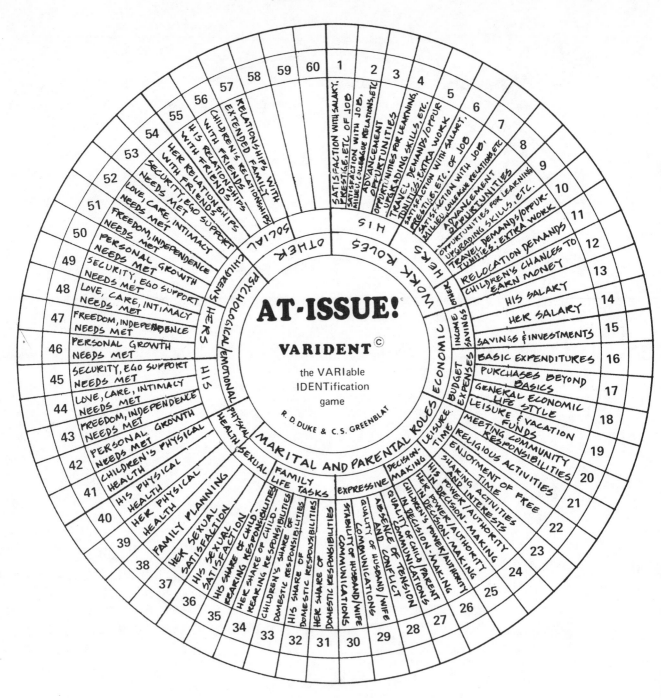

INSTRUCTIONS FOR PLAY

Assess the impact on each variable using this scale:

+2   make things much better
+1   make things a little better
 0   no effect
−1   make things a little worse
−2   make things much worse

On the reverse side add any comments you consider appropriate.

CONCEPTUAL MAPPING GAME... EXAMPLES

Overview.

Three examples of the CONCEPTUAL MAPPING GAME... are included here:

Regional Planning CONCEPTUAL MAPPING GAME... by Nina Binin and Michael Hanau. This was originally prepared for use in Monterey Bay, California, and has subsequently been employed in other areas. To use it requires:

a. A copy of the problem description from Regional Planning AT-ISSUE!

b. A set of issue cards from Regional Planning AT-ISSUE! if a small group is participating; otherwise use one set for each group of 7-8 people.

c. For a small group, use one copy of the conceptual map for each issue. When playing with a large group, use a copy of the conceptual map for central recording, and a copy for each issue considered which will be cut up and divided among the groups (with 7-10 members per group).

d. If several issues are being considered, use a "master" conceptual map for central recording of cumulative impacts.

2. Criminal Justice System CONCEPTUAL MAPPING GAME... by Cathy S. Greenblat and Richard M. Stephenson. This map was originally created for use in a workshop on changing dimensions of the criminal justice system. It is presented here with a few sample issues that might be considered by a group interested in this topic. Play requires the maps (as above) and the list of issues or any other event that can be fruitfully linked with the variable set.

3. Public School System CONCEPTUAL MAPPING GAME... by Barbara Goldberg. This was prepared for this manual as a game for those concerned with issues involving the public schools. It is playable by administrators, school board members, faculty, students or by a combination of the members of these groups. Play requires the maps (listed above) and the sample issues, either those listed in this manual or your own.

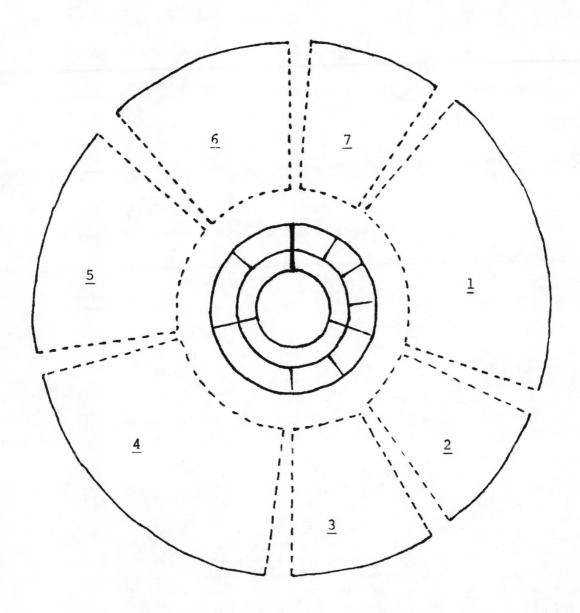

This is the schematic layout for the "Regional Planning" CONCEPTUAL
MAPPING GAME wheel. Refer to this page when assembling the wheel.
The different pieces for the wheel are on the following eight pages.

This page and the next seven pages constitute the "Regional Planning" CONCEPTUAL MAPPING GAME wheel. Cut out this small circle. Place in the center of a table. Cut out the pieces of the rest of the circle on the following seven pages and line them up with this circle following the directions on each page. Refer to the main diagram on the preceding page for the schematic layout.

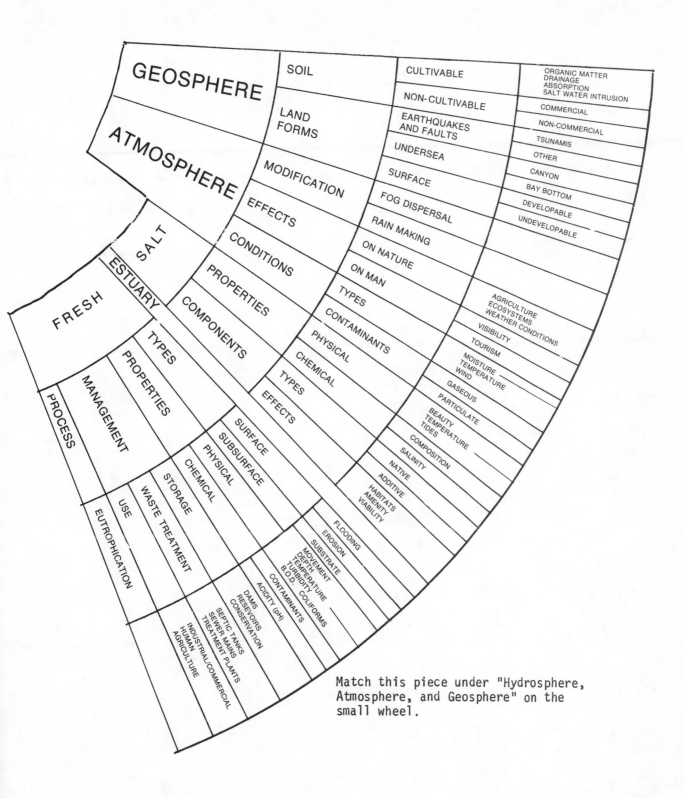

GEOSPHERE

ATMOSPHERE

SALT

ESTUARY

FRESH

SOIL
- CULTIVABLE
  - ORGANIC MATTER
  - DRAINAGE
  - ABSORPTION
  - SALT WATER INTRUSION
- NON-CULTIVABLE
  - COMMERCIAL
  - NON-COMMERCIAL

LAND FORMS
- EARTHQUAKES AND FAULTS
  - TSUNAMIS
  - OTHER
- UNDERSEA
  - CANYON
  - BAY BOTTOM

MODIFICATION
- SURFACE
  - DEVELOPABLE
  - UNDEVELOPABLE
- FOG DISPERSAL

EFFECTS
- RAIN MAKING
- ON NATURE
- ON MAN

CONDITIONS
- TYPES
  - AGRICULTURE
  - ECOSYSTEMS
  - WEATHER CONDITIONS
  - VISIBILITY
  - TOURISM

PROPERTIES
- CONTAMINANTS
  - MOISTURE
  - TEMPERATURE
  - WIND

COMPONENTS
- PHYSICAL
  - GASEOUS
  - PARTICULATE
- CHEMICAL
  - BEAUTY
  - TEMPERATURE
  - TIDES

TYPES
- COMPOSITION
- SALINITY
- NATIVE
- ADDITIVE

EFFECTS
- HABITATS
- AMENITY
- VIABILITY

TYPES
- SURFACE
- SUBSURFACE

PROPERTIES
- PHYSICAL
  - FLOODING
  - EROSION
  - SUBSTRATE
  - MOVEMENT
  - DEPTH
  - TEMPERATURE
  - TURBIDITY
  - B.O.D.
  - COLIFORMS
- CHEMICAL
  - CONTAMINANTS
  - ACIDITY (pH)

MANAGEMENT
- STORAGE
  - DAMS
  - RESERVOIRS
  - CONSERVATION
- WASTE TREATMENT
  - SEPTIC TANKS
  - SEWER MAINS
  - TREATMENT PLANTS

PROCESS
- USE
- EUTROPHICATION
  - INDUSTRIAL/COMMERCIAL
  - HUMAN
  - AGRICULTURE

Match this piece under "Hydrosphere, Atmosphere, and Geosphere" on the small wheel.

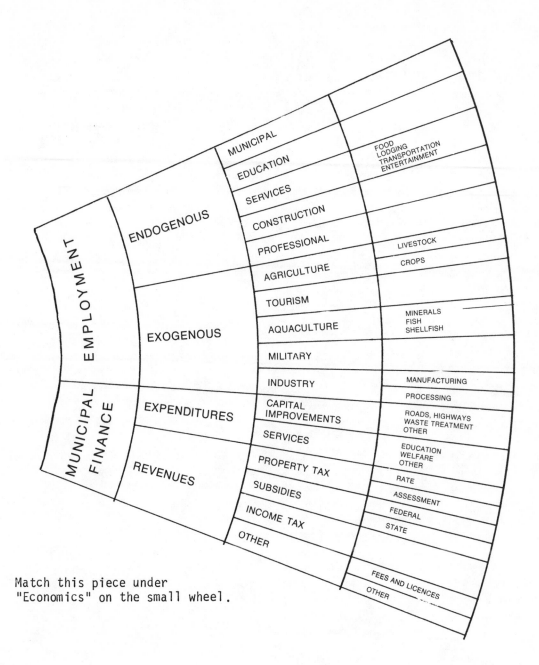

Match this piece under
"Economics" on the small wheel.

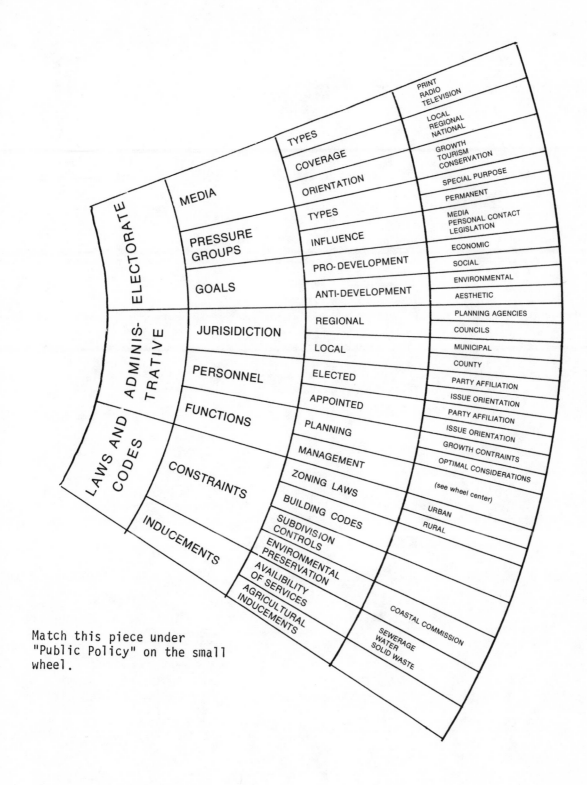

Match this piece under
"Public Policy" on the small
wheel.

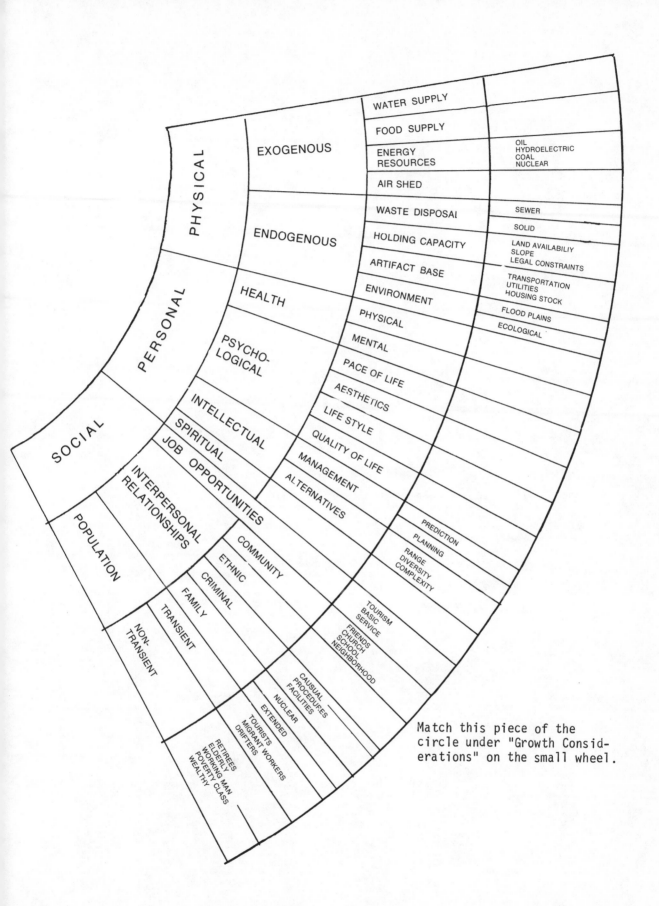

Match this piece of the circle under "Growth Considerations" on the small wheel.

The labels visible in the wheel diagram, from top to bottom:

PHYSICAL — EXOGENOUS: WATER SUPPLY, FOOD SUPPLY, ENERGY RESOURCES (OIL, HYDROELECTRIC, COAL, NUCLEAR), AIR SHED

PHYSICAL — ENDOGENOUS: WASTE DISPOSAL (SEWER, SOLID), HOLDING CAPACITY (LAND AVAILABILIY, SLOPE, LEGAL CONSTRAINTS), ARTIFACT BASE (TRANSPORTATION, UTILITIES, HOUSING STOCK)

PERSONAL — HEALTH: ENVIRONMENT (FLOOD PLAINS, ECOLOGICAL), PHYSICAL, MENTAL

PERSONAL — PSYCHO-LOGICAL: PACE OF LIFE, AESTHETICS, LIFE STYLE

PERSONAL — INTELLECTUAL, SPIRITUAL: QUALITY OF LIFE, MANAGEMENT, ALTERNATIVES

PERSONAL — JOB OPPORTUNITIES: PREDICTION, PLANNING, RANGE, DIVERSITY, COMPLEXITY

SOCIAL — INTERPERSONAL RELATIONSHIPS: COMMUNITY, ETHNIC, CRIMINAL, FAMILY; TOURISM, BASIC, SERVICE; FRIENDS, CHURCH, SCHOOL, NEIGHBORHOOD

SOCIAL — POPULATION: TRANSIENT, NON-TRANSIENT; CAUSUAL, PROCEDURES, FACILITIES; NUCLEAR, EXTENDED; TOURISTS, MIGRANT WORKERS, DRIFTERS; RETIREES, ELDERLY, WORKING MAN, POVERTY CLASS, WEALTHY

-101-

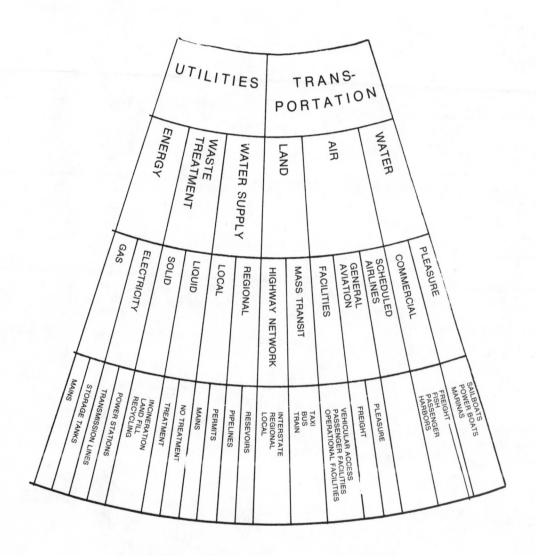

Match this piece under "Infrastructure" on the
small wheel.

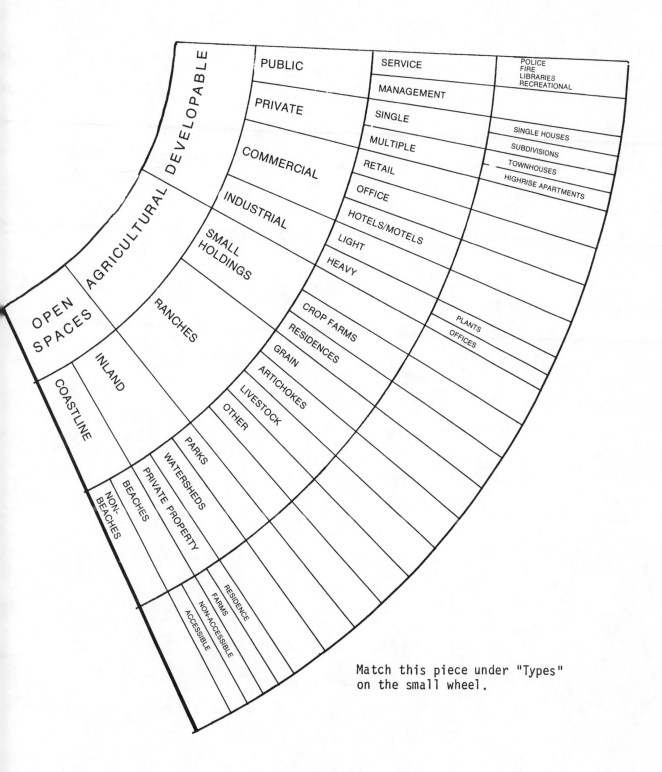

PUBLIC — SERVICE — POLICE / FIRE / LIBRARIES / RECREATIONAL

MANAGEMENT

PRIVATE — SINGLE — SINGLE HOUSES

MULTIPLE — SUBDIVISIONS

COMMERCIAL — RETAIL — TOWNHOUSES

OFFICE — HIGHRISE APARTMENTS

INDUSTRIAL — HOTELS/MOTELS

SMALL HOLDINGS — LIGHT

HEAVY

RANCHES — CROP FARMS — PLANTS

RESIDENCES — OFFICES

GRAIN

INLAND — ARTICHOKES

LIVESTOCK

OPEN SPACES — OTHER

COASTLINE — PARKS

WATERSHEDS

PRIVATE PROPERTY

BEACHES

NON-BEACHES — RESIDENCE

FARMS

NON-ACCESSIBLE

ACCESSIBLE

AGRICULTURAL

DEVELOPABLE

Match this piece under "Types"
on the small wheel.

-105-

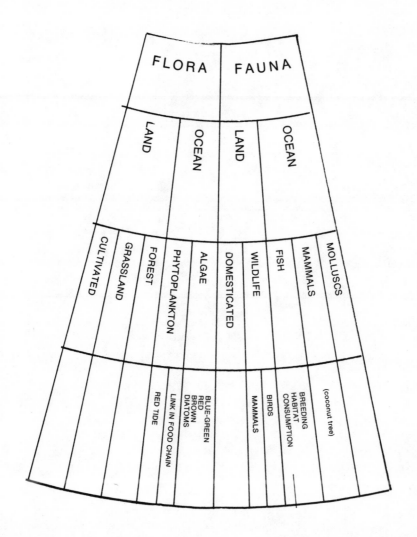

Match this piece under "Biosphere" on the
small wheel.

Criminal Justice System CONCEPTUAL MAPPING GAME...

Cathy S. Greenblat and Richard M. Stephenson

Description of the Problem.

The system for dispensing criminal justice in the Unites States is one comprised of four major segments. First, there are those units charged with defining what is and what is not a crime. Some acts are considered crimes in all states, while others are "criminal" in some and not other jurisdictions. Similarly, the severity of a particular act (e.g., misdemeanor or felony) frequently differs from one jurisdiction to another, and whether an act is a crime may also depend on the age of the offender. As definitions of "crime" change, so do the people labeled "criminals."

The second segment of the criminal justice system consists of those concerned with the identification and apprehension of those who are involved in crime. These law enforcement agents are police, the FBI, private detectives, etc. and are sometimes supplemented by citizen groups.

The third segment is concerned with judicial process: determining whether the apprehended person is to be considered guilty of the crime of which he or she is accused. There are a number of component parts to this segment, depending again on the type of crimeand on the regulations and procedures of the jurisdiction.

Finally, there is a segment concerned with corrections, or doling out the punishments and rehabilitative measures ordered at the conclusion of the adjudication procedure. Institutions for this function include not only full confinement institutions (prisons), but also special treatment centers and parole agencies.

Alterations in any one of these segments - i.e., in definitions of crimes and offenders, or in the processes of law enforcement, adjudication or corrections - are likely to alter aspects of the other segments. This CONCEPTUA

MAPPING GAME... is designed to provide a way of exploring the interconnections.

Select one of the events and follow the directions for play.

Instructions for Play.

General instructions for play are found in section II. Using one or sever.

of the issues below or some of your own making, follow the directions. The sca

is:

+2 or yellow Makes things much **better**
+1 or orange Makes things a little better
 0 or white   No effect
-1 or green   Makes things a little worse
-2 or blue   Makes things much worse

Issues.

1. The State Legislature in your state has just altered the laws of your
    state, defining drug addiction as a medical problem rather than a
    criminal problem. Addicts are going to be able to receive maintenance
    doses of the drugs to which they are addicted at a modest cost. The
    purpose is to prevent the need to resort to crime to obtain money for
    drug purchase, and to reduce the traffic in illegal drugs. Physicians
    will avoid giving drugs solely for the gratification of the person
    requesting them. What would you expect the impact to be on the elemen
    in the CONCEPTUAL MAPPING GAME... wheel?

2. In order to attempt to deal with rising crime rates, the mayor of the
    capital city of your state has just announced a plan to double the
    police force's foot and car patrol units around the clock. What impac
    do you think this will have on the elements on the CONCEPTUAL MAPPING
    GAME... wheel?

3. A series of measures have been taken to make jury duty requirements mo
    stringent and more strictly enforced. As a result, the proportion of
    middle-class, well-educated men and women serving on juries in your st
    has increased markedly. What impact will this have on the elements in
    the CONCEPTUAL MAPPING GAME... wheel?

4. The prisons of your state have received funds to permit the introducti
    in all prisons of personnel trained in psychiatric and psychological
    counciling so that every inmate will have available to him one hour a
    week of counciling services. What do you think the impacts will be
    after one year?

-110-

This page and the next eight pages constitute the "Criminal
Justice System" CONCEPTUAL MAPPING GAME wheel. Cut out this
small circle. Place in the center of a table. Cut out the
pieces of the rest of the circle on the following eight pages
and line them up with this circle. Follow the directions on
each page.

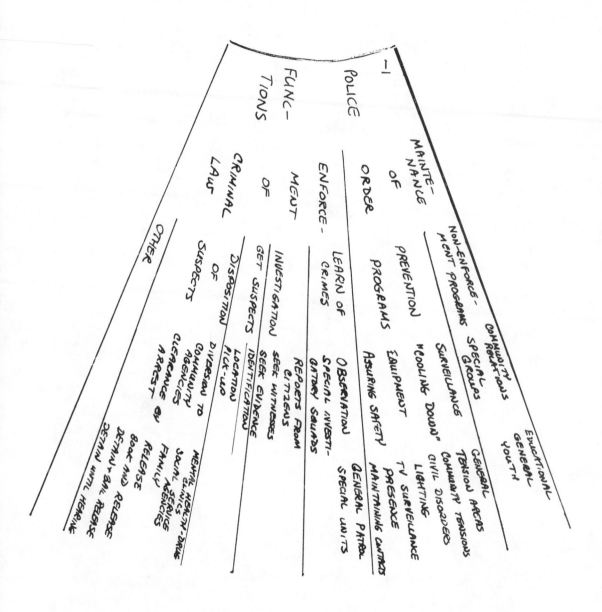

Cut out this piece of the circle. Notice the number "1" in the
upper right-hand corner of the piece. Match this number with
the number "1" located on the small wheel under "Law Enforcement."

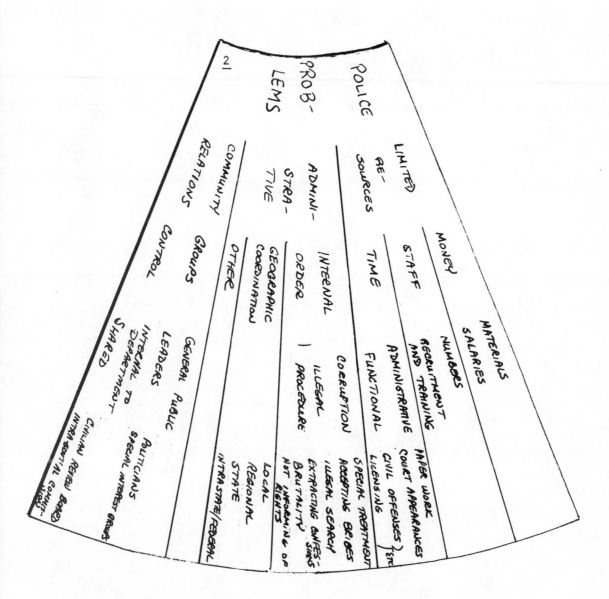

The figure contains the following handwritten labels (read as a fan-shaped wheel segment):

2

POLICE PROB- LEMS

LIMITED RE- SOURCES	MONEY	MATERIALS SALARIES	
	STAFF	NUMBERS	RECRUITMENT AND TRAINING
	TIME	ADMINISTRATIVE	PAPER WORK COURT APPEARANCES CIVIL OFFENSES LICENSING (ETC
ADMINI- STRA- TIVE	INTERNAL ORDER	FUNCTIONAL	SPECIAL TREATMENT
		CORRUPTION	ACCEPTING BRIBES ILLEGAL SEARCH
	ILLEGAL PROCEDURE		BRUTALITY EXTRACTING CONFES- SIONS NOT INFORMING OF RIGHTS
	GEOGRAPHIC COORDINATION		LOCAL REGIONAL STATE INTRASTATE/FEDERAL
	OTHER		
COMMUNITY RELATIONS GROUPS	GENERAL PUBLIC LEADERS		POLITICIANS SPECIAL INTEREST GROUPS
	CONTROL	INTERNAL TO DEPARTMENT	CIVILIAN REVIEW BOARD INTRA-DEPT'AL COMMIT- TEES
	SHARED		

Cut out this piece of the circle. Notice the number "2" in the left hand corner of the piece. Match this number with the number "2" located on the small wheel under "Law Enforcement."

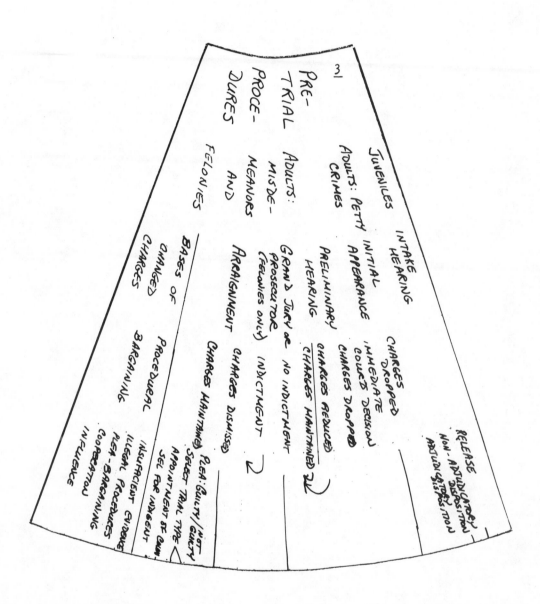

Cut out this piece of the circle. Notice the number "3" in the upper right-hand corner of the piece. Match this number with the number "3" located on the small wheel under "Adjudication."

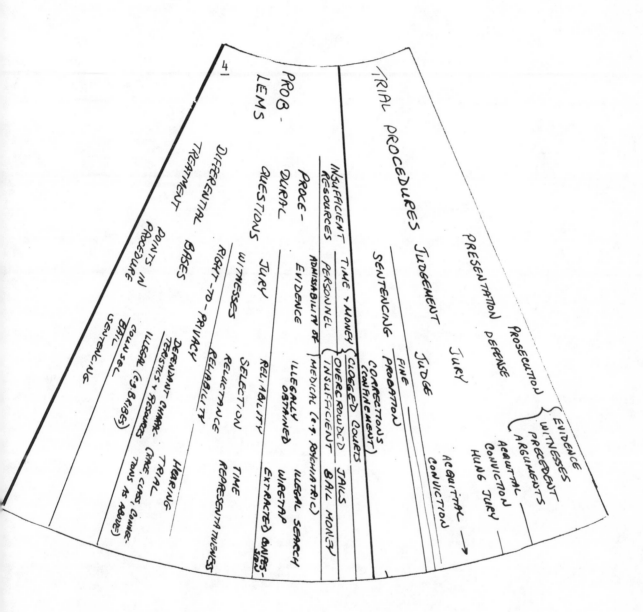

Cut out this piece of the circle. Notice the number "4" in the upper left-hand corner of the piece. Match this number with the number "4" located on the small wheel under "Adjudication."

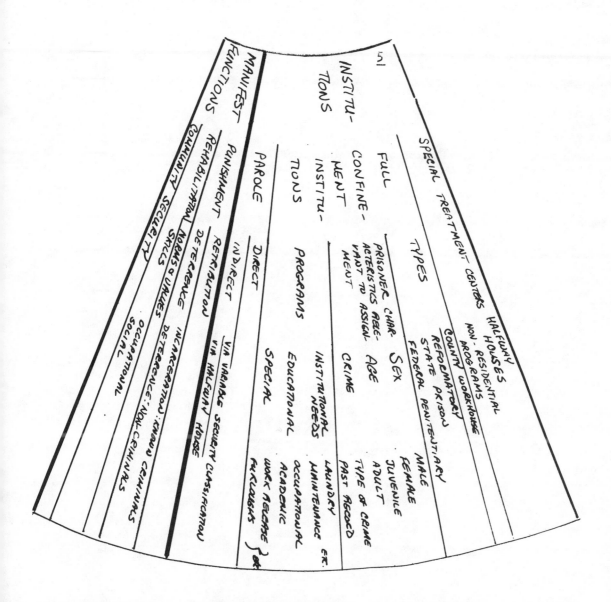

Cut out this piece of the circle. Notice the number "5" in the upper right-hand corner of the piece. Match this number with the number "5" located on the small wheel under "Corrections."

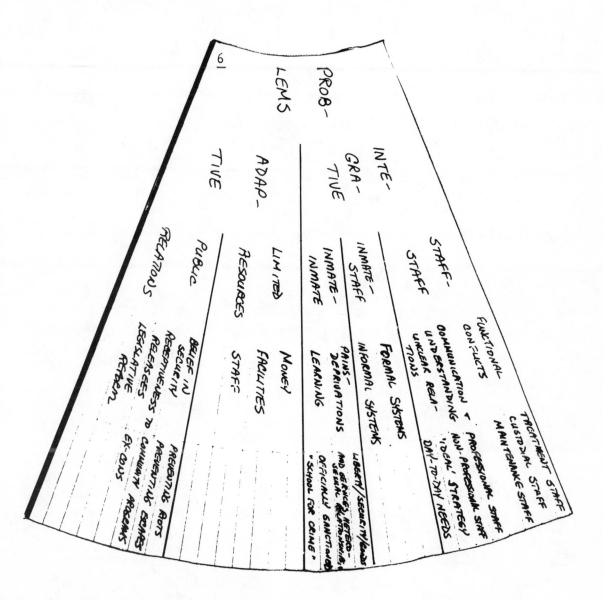

Cut out this piece of the circle. Notice the number "6" in the upper
left-hand corner of the piece. Match this number with the number "6"
located on the small wheel under "Corrections."

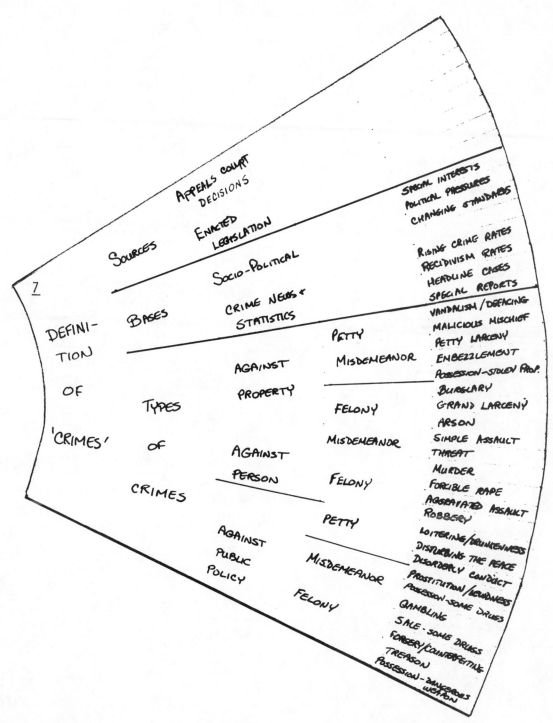

7

DEFINI-
TION

OF

'CRIMES'

Sources — Appeals court decisions
Enacted Legislation

Bases — Socio-Political — Special interests / Political pressures / Changing standards
Crime News & Statistics — Rising crime rates / Recidivism rates / Headline cases / Special reports

Types

of

Crimes

Against Property
- Petty — Misdemeanor — Vandalism / Defacing / Malicious Mischief / Petty Larceny / Embezzlement / Possession - Stolen Prop.
- Felony — Burglary / Grand Larceny / Arson

Against Person
- Misdemeanor — Simple Assault / Threat
- Felony — Murder / Forcible Rape / Aggravated Assault / Robbery

Against Public Policy
- Petty — Misdemeanor — Loitering / Drunkenness / Disturbing the Peace / Disorderly Conduct / Prostitution / Lewdness / Possession - Some Drugs
- Felony — Gambling / Sale - Some Drugs / Forgery / Counterfeiting / Treason / Possession - Dangerous Weapon

Cut out this piece of the circle. Notice the number "7" in the
upper right-hand corner of the piece. Match this number with the
number "7" located on the small wheel under "Crimes and Offenders."

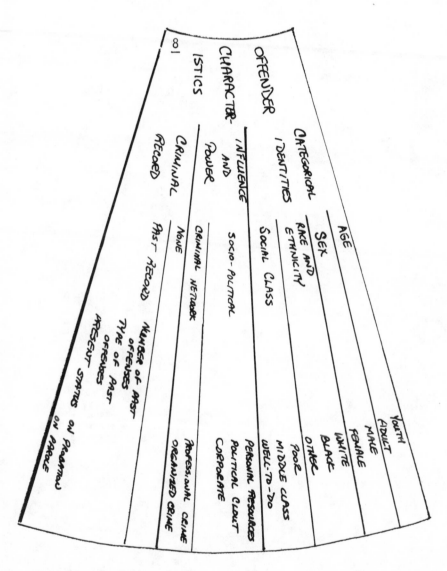

Cut out this piece of the circle. Notice the number "8" in the
upper left-hand corner of the piece. Match this number with the
number "8" located on the small wheel under "Crimes and Offenders."

Public School System CONCEPTUAL MAPPING GAME...

Description of the Problem.

The Public School System is a uniquely important part of our society. All of the population has contact with it; and, in a typical municipality, frequently more than two thirds of all public monies are spent on it. Today, school systems are facing many difficult and controversial problems. Many people are calling for changes - in its structure, procedures, curricula and programs, teaching methods, reward systems, etc. This CONCEPTUAL MAPPING GAME... wheel identifies some variables in the public school system. Select the issues from those listed below or invent issues of your own.

Issues.

1. Women are encouraged to join all intermural sports programs, and are rewarded when they do so. What will be the impact on:

2. All subject matter requirements for a high school diploma are abolished. What will be the impact on:

3. The state mandates an open-enrollment policy, on a first-come, first-serve basis, to all state colleges and universities. What will be the impact on:

4. An alternative (open) high school has been started within the school system. It is capable of serving ten percent of the student body. What will be the impact on:

5. A program of cross-district bussing to achieve racial balance is instituted on the elementary and secondary level. What will be the impact on:

6. Teachers unionize and negotiate their contracts by collective bargaining. What will be the impact on:

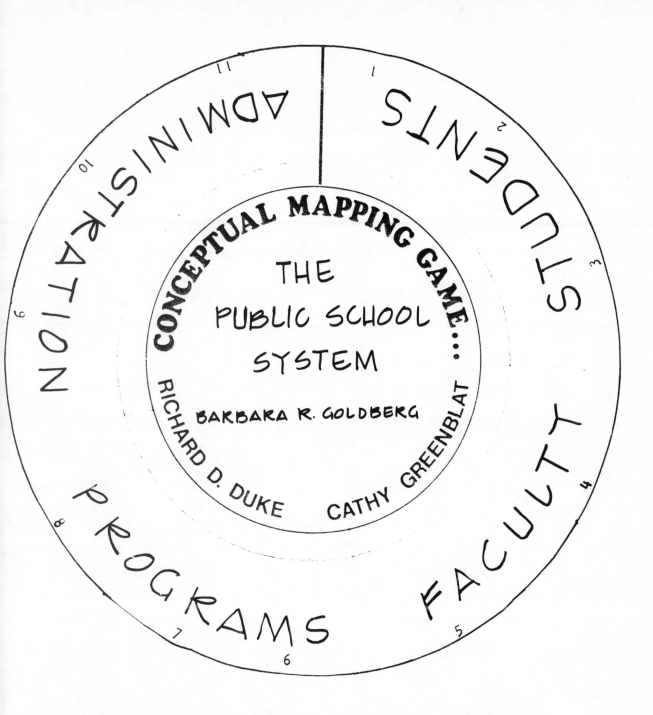

This page and the next eleven pages constitute the "Public School
System" CONCEPTUAL MAPPING GAME wheel. Cut out this small circle.
Place in the center of a table. Cut out the pieces of the rest of
the wheel on the following eleven pages. Line up the numbers
located on the top of each piece with the corresponding numbers
on this wheel. When finished, the completed wheel will be assembled.

PHYSICAL DEVELOPMENT

1

SENSES
- HEARING
- VISUAL
- SPEECH

MUSCULAR COORDINATION
- MANUAL DEXTERITY
- OVERALL

FITNESS
- FLEXIBILITY
- STRENGTH
- STAMINA

NUTRITIONAL STATE
- QUANTITY FOOD AVAILABLE
- QUALITY FOOD AVAILABLE

ACADEMIC DEVELOPMENT

SCHOOL

STUDENT/ ADMINISTRATION RELATIONS
- RULES OF CONDUCT
- ATTENDANCE
- POLICY INPUT
- MISCELLANEOUS

EXTRA-CURRICULAR
- ACTIVITIES
- STUDENT ORGANIZATIONS — STUDENT GOVERNMENT, ACADEMIC CLUBS

STUDENT/ FACULTY RELATIONS
- DISCIPLINE
- STUDENT/FACULTY RATIO
- INPUT TO CURRICULUM CONTENT

CLASSROOM

CURRICULUM
- ACADEMIC PROGRESS — READING ABILITY, WRITING ABILITY, MATH ABILITY, RATE OF PROGRESS
- REQUIREMENTS FOR GRADUATION
- CHOICE OF CLASSES
- CHOICE OF PROGRAMS

3

SOCIAL-
PSYCHOLOGICAL
DEVELOPMENT

INTERPERSONAL

INDIVIDUAL

SOCIAL
ATTITUDES

GROUP
IDENTIFICATION

TEAMWORK
SKILLS

PEER
RELATIONSHIPS

INDIVIDUAL
IDENTITY

SENSE OF
COMPETENCE

SENSE OF
RESPONSIBILITY

FEELING OF
BELONGING

PERSONAL
VALUES

SELF-DISCIPLINE

CREATIVITY

SPONTANEITY

RACISM / SEXISM

MISC. PREJUDICES

ETHNIC
PEER
SCHOOL
COMMUNITY

-137-

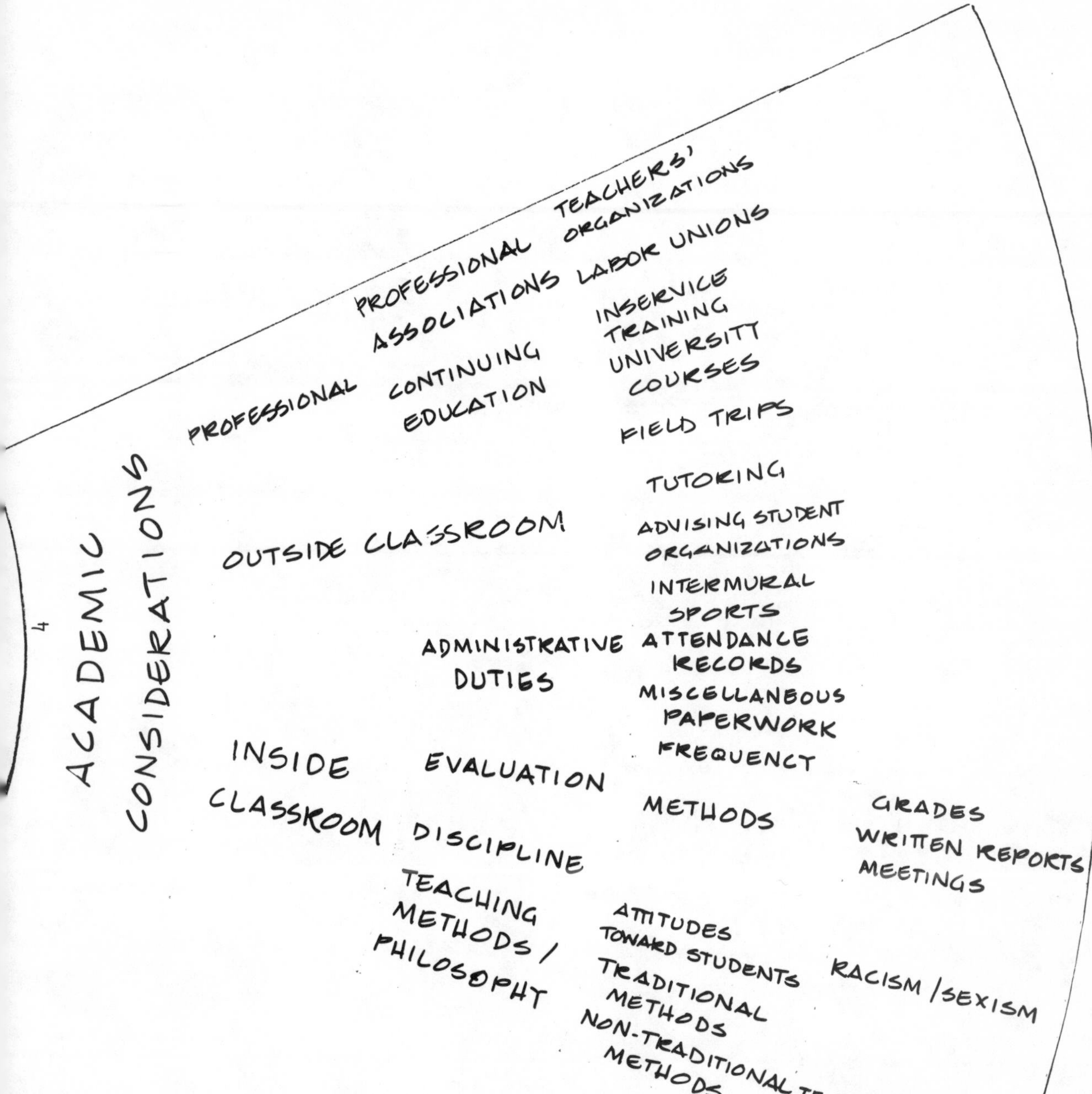

ACADEMIC CONSIDERATIONS

PROFESSIONAL

TEACHERS' ORGANIZATIONS

ASSOCIATIONS LABOR UNIONS

CONTINUING EDUCATION

INSERVICE TRAINING

UNIVERSITY COURSES

FIELD TRIPS

TUTORING

OUTSIDE CLASSROOM

ADVISING STUDENT ORGANIZATIONS

INTERMURAL SPORTS

ADMINISTRATIVE DUTIES

ATTENDANCE RECORDS

MISCELLANEOUS PAPERWORK

FREQUENCY

INSIDE CLASSROOM

EVALUATION

DISCIPLINE

METHODS

GRADES

WRITTEN REPORTS

MEETINGS

TEACHING METHODS / PHILOSOPHY

ATTITUDES TOWARD STUDENTS

TRADITIONAL METHODS

NON-TRADITIONAL METHODS

RACISM / SEXISM

TEAM-TEACHING

OPEN CLASSROOM

5

EMPLOYMENT CONSIDERATIONS

CONDITIONS OF EMPLOYMENT PROFESSIONAL

ECONOMIC

CLASSROOM
- FACULTY/STUDENT RATIO
- DETERMINATION OF CURRICULUM CONTENT

LEGAL REQUIREMENTS
- TENURE
- RESIDENCY LAWS
- NUMBER OF WORKING DAYS/YR
- AGE OF RETIREMENT

DISCIPLINARY
- DUE PROCESS
- SEVERANCE POLICIES

FRINGE BENEFITS
- VACATION PAY
- SICK PAY
- RETIREMENT
- INSURANCE

BASIC SALARY STRUCTURE
- COST OF LIVING INCREASES
- INCREMENTAL ADVANCEMENT

6

SUPPORT SERVICES

GENERAL SUPPORT

- TECHNICAL
  - ADMINISTRATIVE
    - BOARD OF EDUCATION
    - RECRUITMENT/REPLACEMENT
    - GENERAL
    - DATA PROCESSING
    - FINANCIAL ACCOUNTING
    - OPERATION OF PLANT
    - FOOD SERVICE
    - TRANSPORT SERVICE

PUPIL SUPPORT

- PHYSICAL
  - HEALTH
  - SPEECH PATHOLOGY
  - AUDIOLOGY
  - VISUAL HANDICAP
- SOCIAL-PSYCHOLOGICAL
  - GUIDANCE
  - PSYCHOLOGICAL
  - SOCIAL WORK

INSTRUCTIONAL SUPPORT

- LIBRARY
  - INSTRUCTION
  - CURRICULUM/DEVELOPMENT
  - AUDIO-VISUAL DEVELOPMENT
  - AUDIO-VISUAL SERVICES

SPECIAL INSTRUCTION

CONTINUING

MENTALLY RETARDED
EMOTIONALLY DISTURBED
LEARNING DISABILITIES
SPECIAL WORKSHOP
WORK-STUDY

EDUCABLE
TRAINABLE

SHORT-TERM

SUMMER SCHOOL
HOMEBOUND INSTRUCTION

8

REGULAR INSTRUCTION

NON-ACADEMIC

ACADEMIC

EXTRA CURRICULAR

PHYSICAL EDUCATION

PRE COLLEGE

TECHNICAL

BUSINESS

STUDENT ORGANIZATION

SOCIAL ACTIVITIES

CURRICULUM

INTERMURAL

FINE ARTS

LANGUAGE ARTS

NATURAL/PHYSICAL SCIENCES

SOCIAL STUDIES

MATHEMATICS

INDUSTRIAL ARTS

HOME ECONOMICS

SEX EDUCATION

HEALTH/NUTRITION

SPORTS

GYMNASTICS

MUSIC

ART

MULTI-CULTURAL PROGRAMS

9

TRICT

BUDGET

EXPENDITURES

PERSONNEL
SALARIES
BENEFITS
LAYOFFS
HIRING

PROGRAMS

PLANT
OPERATION
MAINTENANCE
FEDERAL
STATE
LOCAL

REVENUES
GOVERNMENT
PRIVATE

PHYSICAL PLANT

BUILDINGS
STRUCTURES
QUANTITY
QUALITY
ATHLETIC FIELDS
QUANTITY
QUALITY
PARKING FACILITIES

VEHICLES
SCHOOL BUSES

EQUIPMENT

ACADEMIC EQUIPMENT
AUDIO-VISUAL

NON-ACADEMIC FURNITURE
BOOKS
TEXTBOOKS
LIBRARY

SUPPLIES

DIS

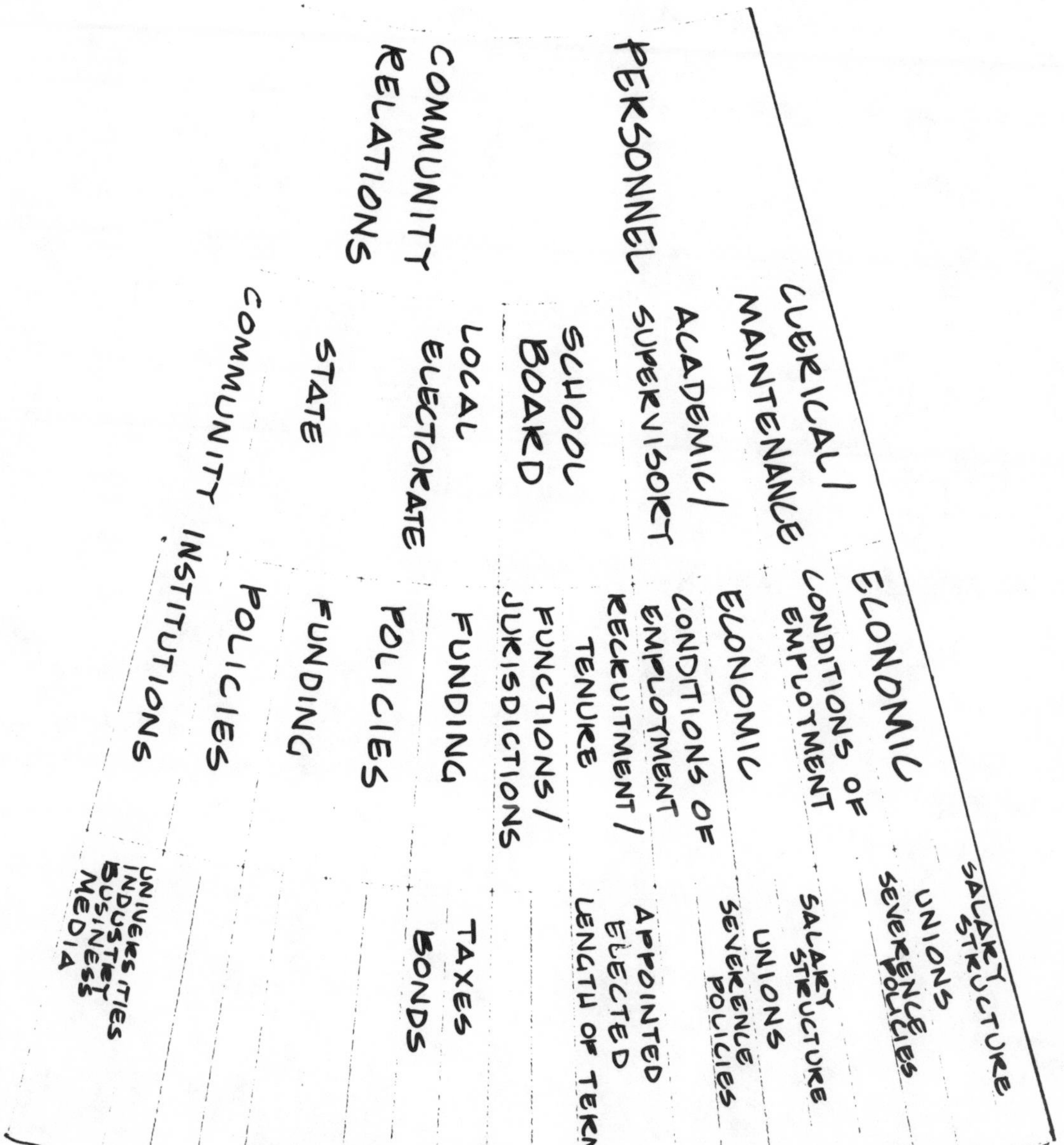

PERSONNEL

CLERICAL/ MAINTENANCE

ACADEMIC/ SUPERVISORY

ECONOMIC

CONDITIONS OF EMPLOYMENT

SALARY STRUCTURE

UNIONS

SEVERENCE POLICIES

ECONOMIC

SALARY STRUCTURE

UNIONS

SEVERENCE POLICIES

CONDITIONS OF EMPLOYMENT

RECRUITMENT/ TENURE

APPOINTED ELECTED LENGTH OF TERM

FUNCTIONS/ JURISDICTIONS

SCHOOL BOARD

LOCAL ELECTORATE

POLICIES

FUNDING

TAXES

BONDS

POLICIES

STATE

FUNDING

POLICIES

COMMUNITY RELATIONS

COMMUNITY INSTITUTIONS

UNIVERSITIES INDUSTRIES BUSINESS MEDIA

11

SCHOOL

ADMINISTRATION/
STUDENT RELATIONS

ADMINISTRATION/
FACULTY RELATIONS

COMMUNITY RELATIONS

PERSONNEL

COUNSELLING

POLICIES

POLICIES

PARENTS

CLERICAL/
MAINTENANCE

ACADEMIC/
SUPERVISORY

COUNSELLORS

ECONOMIC
CONDITIONS OF
EMPLOYMENT

ECONOMIC
CONDITIONS OF
EMPLOYMENT

ECONOMIC
CONDITIONS OF
EMPLOYMENT

CONTIGUOUS
COMMUNITY

TEACHER
TRAINING

DISCIPLINE/
SECURITY

PERSONAL

ACADEMIC/VOCATIONAL

STUDENT INPUT

PUNITIVE

PREVENTIVE

FACULTY INPUT

CROSS-DISTRICT BUSING

USE OF SCHOOL FACILITIES

VI. BLANK FORMS

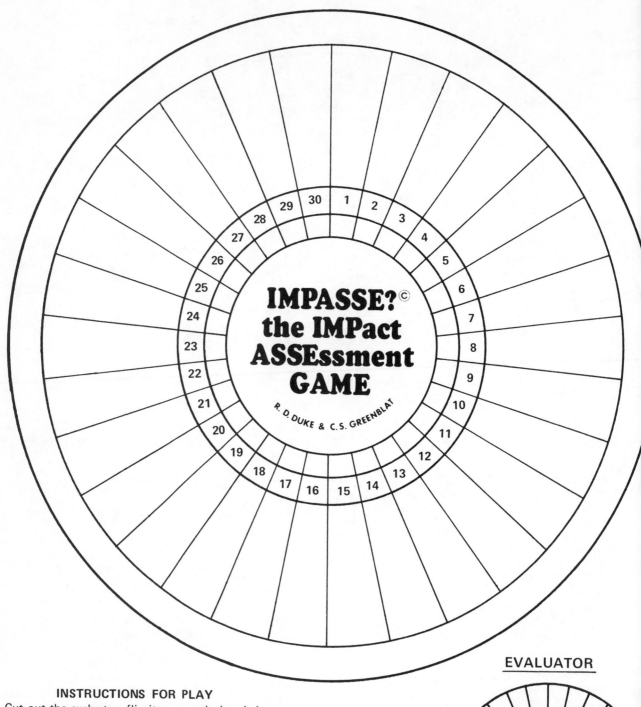

INSTRUCTIONS FOR PLAY

Cut out the evaluator, flip it over, and place it in the center of the game wheel. Assess the impact on each problem using this scale:

A - make things much worse
B - make things a little worse
C - no effect
D - make things a little better
E - make things much better

Record your answers on the game wheel, then flip the evaluator, line up the numbers and compare with the "expert" whose logic is explained on the next page. Play alone or with others.

EVALUATOR

THE
EXPERT'S
OPINION

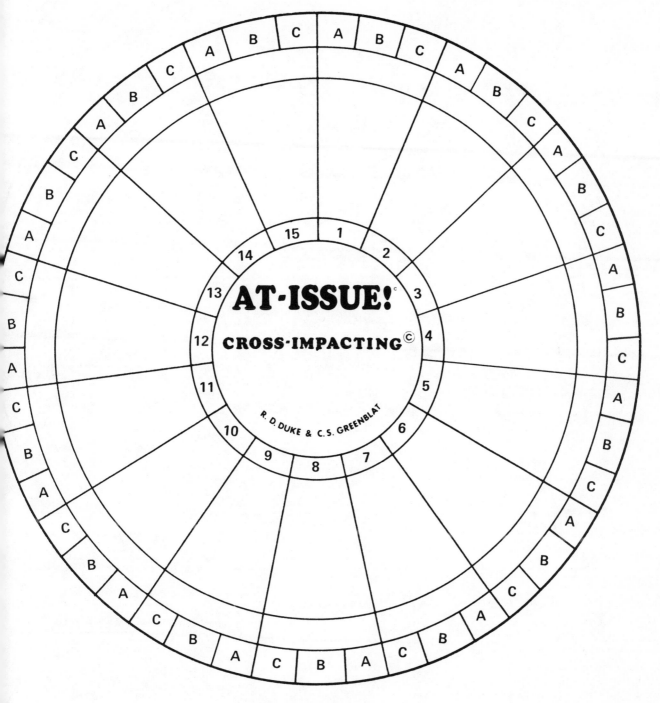

AT-ISSUE!

CROSS-IMPACTING ©

R. D. DUKE & C.S. GREENBLAT

INSTRUCTIONS FOR PLAY

Assess the impact of this issue resolution on all other issues:

A = increased probability of the issue being resolved AFFIRMATIVELY

B = increased probability of the issue being resolved NEGATIVELY

C = NO IMPACT

Issue No. _____   Issue Name _____

_____ Affirmative Resolution   _____ Negative Resolution

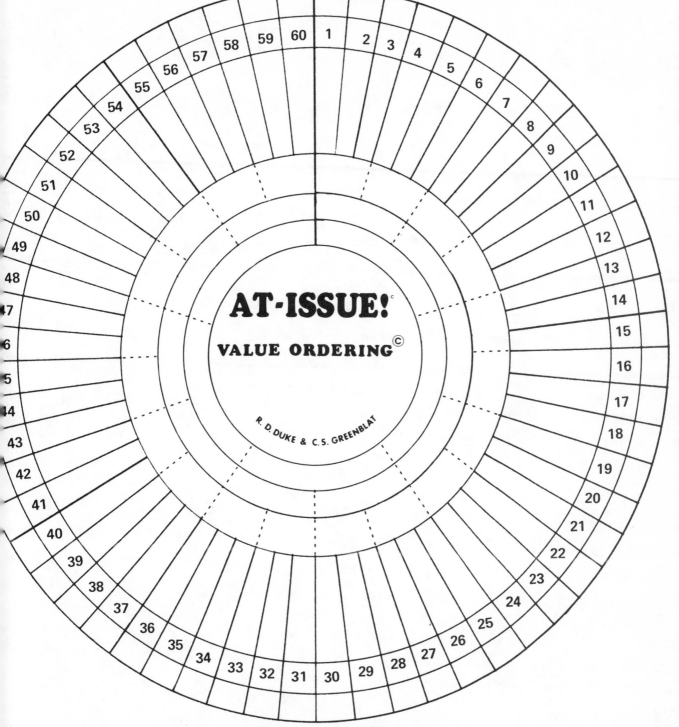

INSTRUCTIONS FOR PLAY

Assign 100 points among the variables, in multiples of 10. These points should indicate the things you most care about. If you would like to see the item increase (e.g., per cent of budget used for schools) put a plus (+) sign in front of your weight. If you would like to see the item decrease (e.g., property tax) put a minus (−) sign in front of the weight

These weights will apply throughout the game so assign them with some care.

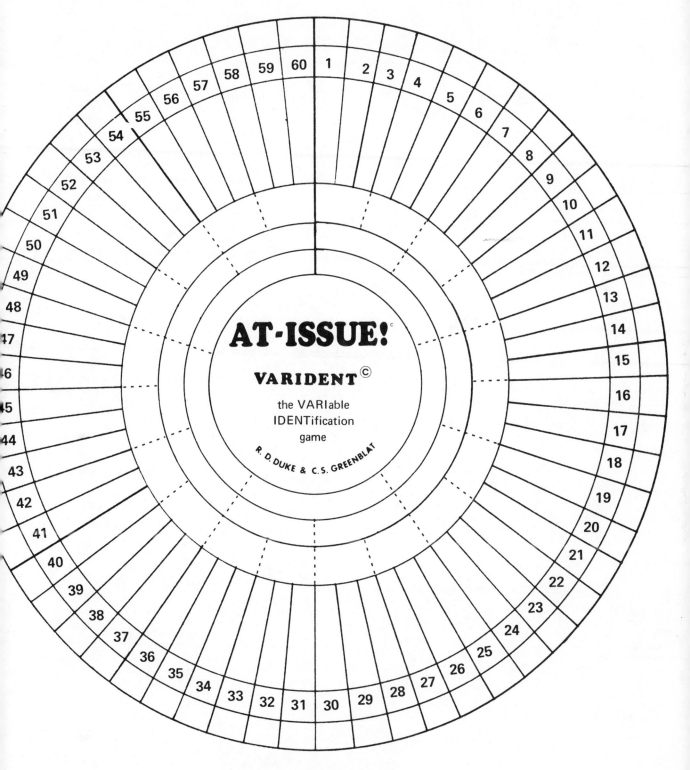

INSTRUCTIONS FOR PLAY

Assess the impact on each variable using this scale:

+2   make things much better
+1   make things a little better
 0   no effect
−1   make things a little worse
−2   make things much worse

On the reverse side add any comments you consider appropriate.

-161-

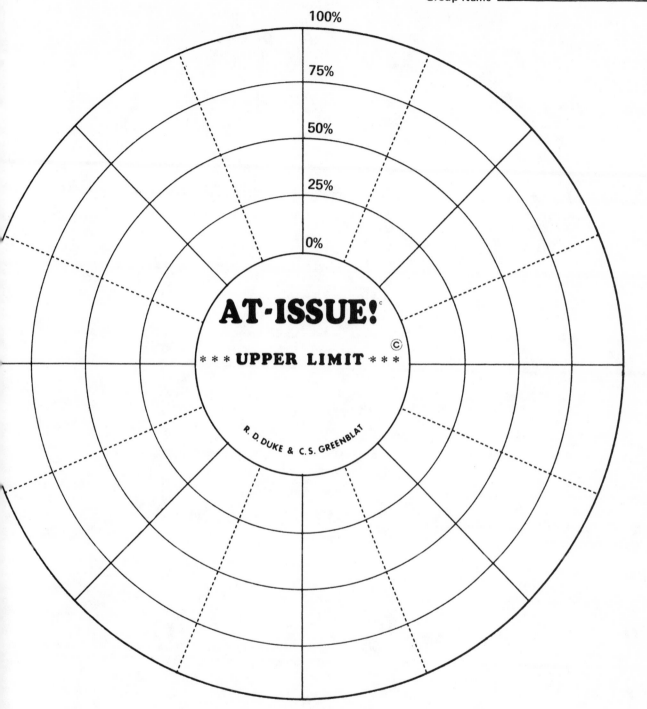

INSTRUCTIONS FOR PLAY

1. Mark each variable to indicate the current level of use
   (to what extent is the system already burdened?). Connect all marks to form a circle.
2. Repeat with a different colored pencil, BUT mark each
   variable as you expect it to be five years from now,
   based on the stated resolution of the issue under discussion.

AT-ISSUE! Perceived Impact Form

roup_____

sue #_____

osition: affirmative resolution____   negative resolution_____

Factor Number	Value Weight (10, 20...)	X	Impact (from VARIDENT) (+2,+1,0,-1,-2)	=	Perceived Impact
_____	_____	X	_____	=	_____
_____	_____	X	_____	=	_____
_____	_____	X	_____	=	_____
_____	_____	X	_____	=	_____
_____	_____	X	_____	=	_____
_____	_____	X	_____	=	_____
_____	_____	X	_____	=	_____
_____	_____	X	_____	=	_____
_____	_____	X	_____	=	_____
_____	_____	X	_____	=	_____
_____	_____	X	_____	=	_____
_____	_____	X	_____	=	_____
_____	_____	X	_____	=	_____
_____	_____	X	_____	=	_____
_____	_____	X	_____	=	_____
_____	_____	X	_____	=	_____
_____	_____	X	_____	=	_____
_____	_____	X	_____	=	_____
_____	_____	X	_____	=	_____
_____	_____	X	_____	=	_____

ur group's total perceived impact on this issue   = _____

rections: Enter the factor number and the value weight for all factors you
           assigned a weight of more than 0. Enter the impacts you assessed
           for these factors in the VARIDENT procedure. Multiply each of
           these and add the Perceived Impact column.

This is a blank CONCEPTUAL MAPPING GAME wheel. It is intended to be used
by the reader when formulating a new game. This page and the next eight
pages constitute the total wheel. Cut out this small circle. Place it in
the center of a table. Cut out the pieces of the rest of the wheel on the
following eight pages. Line up the numbers located at the top of each
piece with the corresponding numbers on this circle. When finished, the
completed wheel will be assembled. Next, write the new issue in the center
circle and fill in the new variables of the game in the outer circles. If
additional "rings" of circles are needed, simply add them on to the outer-
most ring.

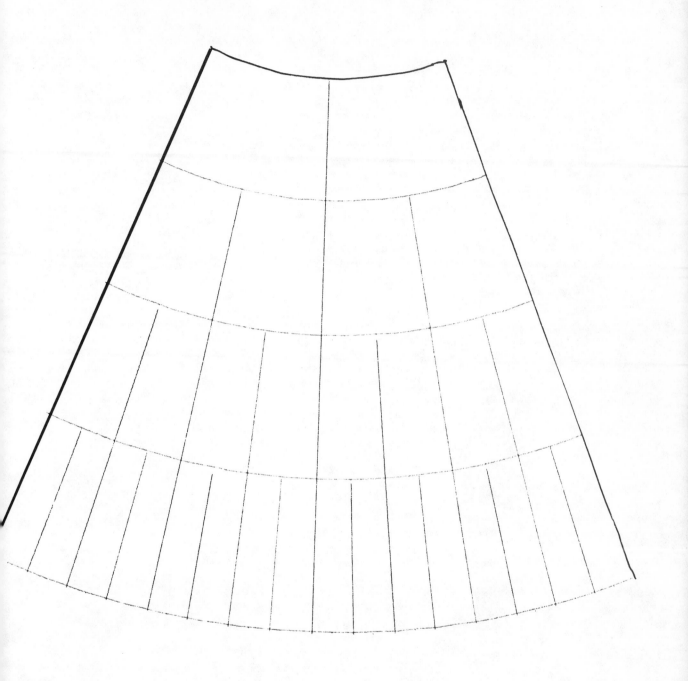

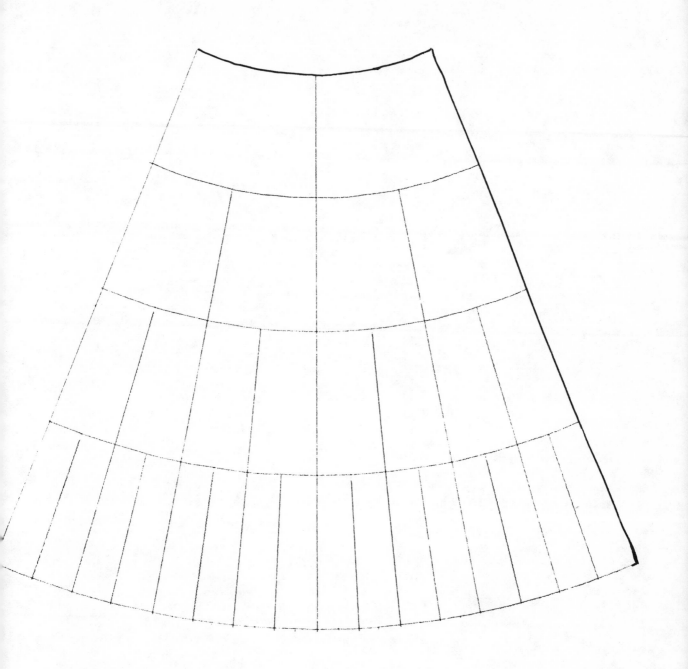

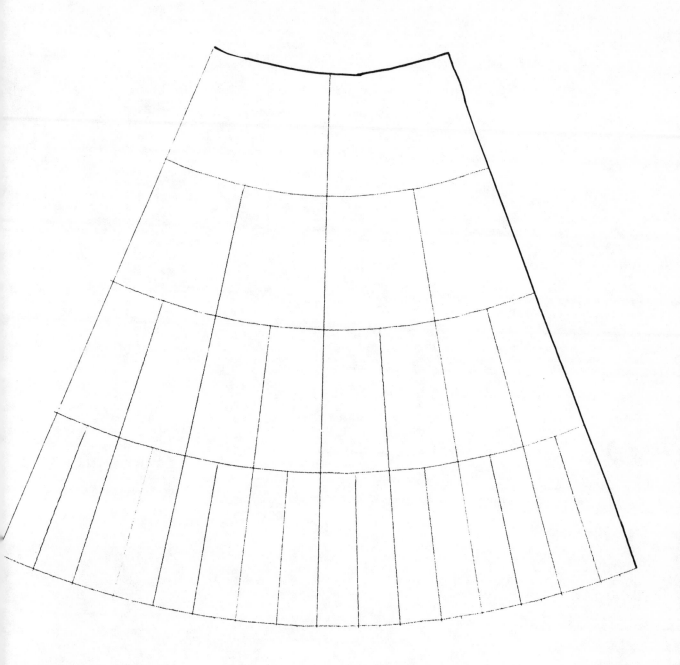

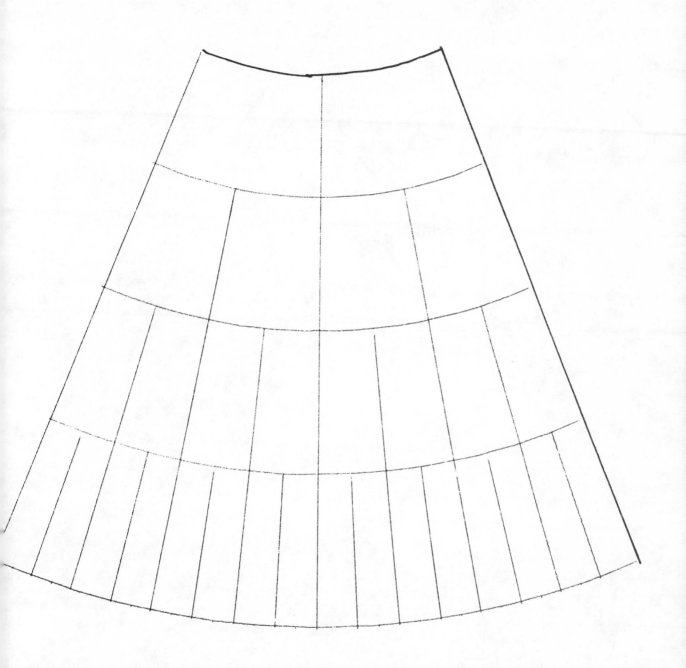

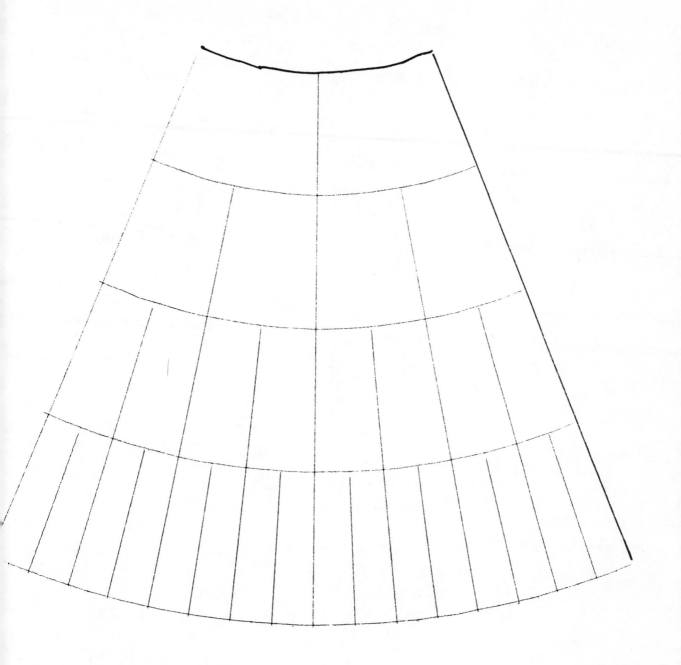

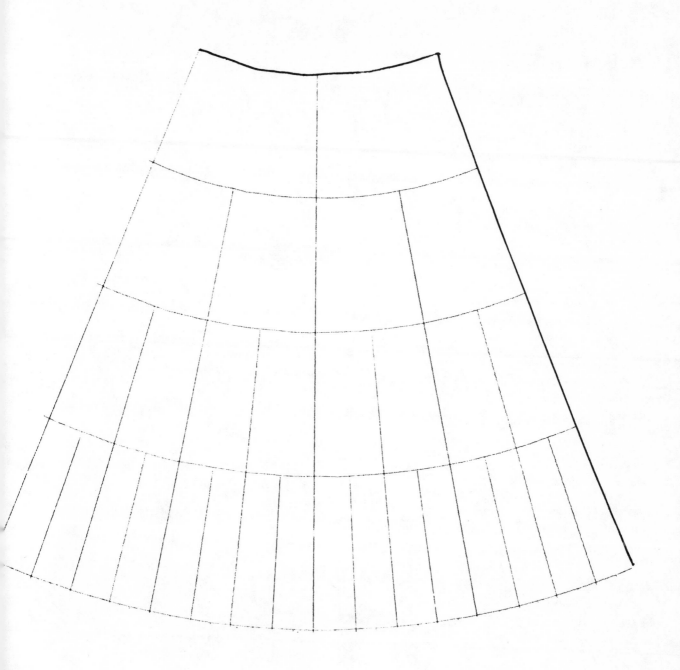

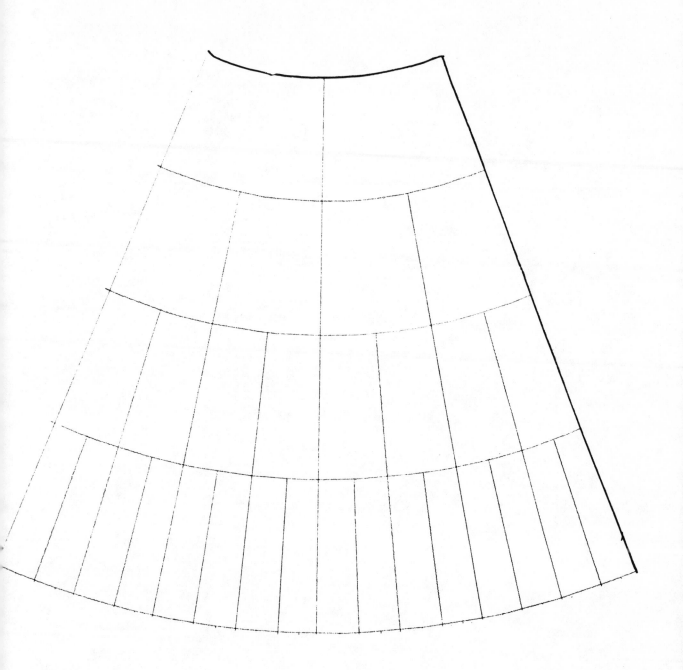

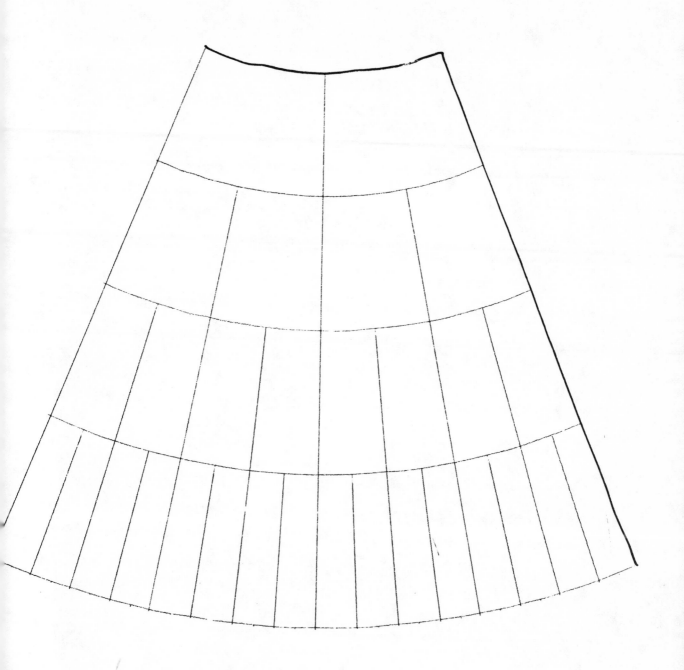

DATE DUE	
MAR 9 1981	AUG 9 1983
	JUN 27 1984
MAR 4 1988	
JUL 30 1988	
OCT 14 1992	
MAR 10 1996	
DEC 0 4 2001	

MP 728